THE WAY TO MIAMI

by

Donald Steele

To my parents,

Fey B. Steele and Mary Alice Steele

and

To Roger Mooney

THE WAY TO MIAMI
by
Donald Steele

with

FRANK . . . . Ron Crawford

LEOLA . . . . Ruth Sherman

Directed by Donald Steele

Originally produced by
The Bridge Theatre Company, Washington Heights, New York

Bryan Wade, Executive Producer

ABOUT THE AUTHOR

DONALD STEELE is a member of The Dramatists Guild and is a Fellow of the MacDowell Colony. He is a graduate of Hope College and The University of Iowa. His full-length play *Graceland* was initially produced at American Stage Festival in 1990, and has received readings across the country. He has written many one-act plays including his one woman piece *Miracle at the Del Mar Boulevard Beauty Salon* which was originally performed by Oscar winner Mercedes Ruehl. His work has been produced several times by The Bridge Theatre Company and he is an active participant with Hudson River Classics in Hudson, New York, where he is a part-time resident.

CHARACTERS

    FRANK: mid 60's
    LEOLA: his wife, 60's

SETTING

    Place: Frank and Leola's kitchen
    Time: Before dawn

(In the dark we hear a man singing and humming a tune. The lights come up on FRANK, in his sixties, sitting at a kitchen table. The kitchen is crowded with cartons packed for moving. FRANK is drinking coffee from one of the two mugs on the table and consulting a highway map. He wears a brightly colored Hawaiian type shirt. LEOLA enters, also in her sixties, wearing a caftan like robe, adjusting an earring. She goes to one of the packed cartons, picks it up, sets it on the table, and begins unpacking it.)

FRANK. What are you doing?
LEOLA. Looking for a cup.
FRANK. I got cups out.
LEOLA. I want one of my nice dinner cups.
FRANK. I got out the mugs.
LEOLA. You drink it out of a mug. I want one of my nice dinner cups. Hold this.

(She hands him a stack of plates wrapped in newspaper.)

FRANK. Don't unpack all of this to find one cup. The movers will be here.

(She continues handing him plates wrapped in paper. She begins to unwrap them as she goes along.)

LEOLA. They aren't here yet. I want the last cup of coffee I'll ever drink in this house to be out of one of my nice china dinner cups. We bought that set for special occasions. This is a special occasion. Not a special occasion like Christmas or Thanksgiving, but I guess some people would call this a special occasion.
FRANK. A lot of people would call moving to Florida a special occasion. I do. It's not every day you move to Florida.

(LEOLA hands him another stack of plates.)

LEOLA. Here. Unwrap these.
FRANK. These are plates. You wanted a cup.
LEOLA. I want to look at the plates again.
FRANK. Why?
LEOLA. I'm going to re-wrap them. I don't like how I wrapped them.
FRANK. You wrapped them just fine.

LEOLA. It's been plaguing me. I want to re-wrap them again.
FRANK. You're making a mess.
LEOLA. We're moving. We have an excuse. What are a few wrinkled papers?
FRANK. A few?

(LEOLA hands him another stack of plates.)

LEOLA. How many is that there?
FRANK. If you wanted to drink your coffee out of one of those nice cups, why'd you pack it?
LEOLA. It crossed my mind, but I thought, "Don't be stupid." I felt silly. Is that five of everything there?

(FRANK looks to count. So does she.)

FRANK. One. Two. Three. Four. Five. Yes. Five. Why?
LEOLA. You. Me. Joanna. Gloria. And Jimmy. Where's a tablecloth?
FRANK. For what?
LEOLA. I want to set the table one more time.
FRANK. Set the table? Now? I told the movers we'd be all ready.
LEOLA. We are.
FRANK. We were. Now we aren't. This is not ready.
LEOLA. So are they pulled up out front? No. Where's the box I put the tablecloths in?
FRANK. You can set the table without a tablecloth.

(She starts looking through some other boxes.)

LEOLA. I always used a tablecloth – oh here it is – whenever I used these dishes. These dishes are meant to be set on a lovely tablecloth. Jimmy gave is this. Put that on. Such good taste.

(FRANK opens the tablecloth and spreads it on the table as LEOLA looks over the dishware making sure she has everything she needs.)

FRANK. We couldn't have done this last night? We couldn't have had a nice dinner on these dishes, on this tablecloth last night? You waited till now?
LEOLA. We could have. But we didn't. With getting everything else ready to go, making sure we were all packed, I wasn't sure there would be time to do this. I'm better organized than I thought. *(She begins laying out the table.)* You here. My spot. Joanna. Gloria. Jimmy's spot. Just like the last time we were all together. Just the five of us. Before anybody got married or ... I was right to pick out these dishes. I knew standing there in

the store, I'd live to regret it if I didn't get these dishes. Give us each a dessert plate and a salad plate. Is that salad plates you got there?

FRANK. What's it matter?

LEOLA. I want to take a picture of the dishes.

FRANK. You have pictures of the dishes.

LEOLA. Not like this.

FRANK. No. But pictures of the dishes at Thanksgiving and you had the table decorated with the wax Pilgrims for each of the kids. And at Christmas time.

LEOLA. So this will be the last of the series. All those other pictures with happy grinning holiday faces in them, and the turkey or the ham in the middle of the table. And this, this is how it ends. *(Pause)* We need a moving van.

FRANK. One is on its way.

LEOLA. For a decoration. The theme of this table is moving. A moving van as a centerpiece and then for place cards, little boxes like packed cartons.

FRANK. Like these used to be.

LEOLA. You sit there. That's your spot and I'll take your picture. Then you take mine. Where's the camera? Get the camera.

FRANK. In the car.

LEOLA. In the car? What's it doing in the car?

FRANK. I want to take some pictures along the way.

LEOLA. Well, go get it.

FRANK. I still have to get some film.

LEOLA. So I'm not the only one who leaves something go till the last minute. *(She looks at the table from different angles. She motions for him to join her.)* Doesn't that look nice?

FRANK. Yes. It looks very nice. *(Pause)* Now put those dishes back in the boxes.

LEOLA. What's the rush?

FRANK. The movers ...

LEOLA. The movers, the movers! If I can't take a picture for real, I'll take a picture of this with my eyes.

FRANK. And then will you pack them?

LEOLA. Sssh. I'm concentrating.

FRANK. You want a cup of coffee while you concentrate?

(LEOLA puts up her hand to silence him. She stares at the dishes and then makes a "clicking" sound as if taking a picture.)

LEOLA. What do you say I make us a nice breakfast? The table's all set. How about that?

FRANK. There's nothing in the refrigerator. We emptied it out.

LEOLA. Well, you run out and get something. How about ham and eggs? French toast? Yeah. Then you can pick up some film. I knew there was a reason we emptied out that refrigerator.

FRANK. Because we're moving. I thought we'd have some coffee. Maybe some toast ...

LEOLA. You have to do these things right. That's no kind of a last meal. Coffee and toast. Even convicts have better last meals.

FRANK. We're not walking the last mile. We're moving to Florida.

LEOLA. You have to leave a place right. It's too dark now. I was hoping to see the house one more time in the daylight.

FRANK. You've had weeks to see the house one more time.

LEOLA. Those times don't count. This is when it counts. You get in the car and look back at the house one more time. In the daylight. It'll be too sad leaving the house in the dark. This is the only house Jimmy ever knew. Or Gloria either. You don't leave a house alone in the dark that's been like that to people. I can't. I don't want to remember our house, have my last look at our house, being left all alone in the dark.

FRANK. It's a house Leola. I wanted to get a good hour or two in on the road before traffic picked up and then stop for some breakfast.

LEOLA. I'm not going.

FRANK. *(Pause)* In the dark.

LEOLA. Or the daylight.

FRANK. The truck is on its way over.

LEOLA. I'm not moving.

FRANK. It'll be here soon.

LEOLA. I'm staying here.

FRANK. Everything else is packed. The house is sold. The Mitchells are moving in on Tuesday. The condominium is waiting for us in Miami.

LEOLA. We can unpack.

FRANK. They're painting the walls. That light green like you wanted. Celery color.

LEOLA. We'll get an apartment here. They have celery color paint here.

FRANK. I made a down payment.

LEOLA. They'll give it back. You changed your mind. You sell it. I'm too used to winter.

FRANK. You wanted summer year round.

LEOLA. So what's that? Dried out baked skin. I'll look like a prune in two weeks. We'll spend a fortune on skin creams. I've never used skin creams. Ever. I'm not starting now.

FRANK. Winter dries out your skin.

LEOLA. It's a different dry.

FRANK. Sun is healthy for you. We get some vitamin from it.

LEOLA. We get skin cancer from it.

FRANK. We were agreed. We discussed this for months. It was all settled.

LEOLA. I gave in.

FRANK. Then it's the first time.

LEOLA. I'm not going. I can't go. I won't know anybody. I won't have any friends.

FRANK. You make some. New ones.

LEOLA. I want the ones I have. The ones who gave us that farewell party. The ones who cried when they found out we were going to Miami. So far away. Almost not even in the country anymore.

FRANK. They'll visit us. They all have our address. The Russells ...

LEOLA. And you know how they'll have to get there? He doesn't see well enough to drive anymore. Fly.

FRANK. *(Slight pause.)* So they fly?

LEOLA. I am not having anyone anymore who I care about fly to see me. No more.

FRANK. Just because they fly doesn't mean ...

LEOLA. You can guarantee it? No. They drive to see me or they don't come.

FRANK. If people want to fly down to see us, we can't tell them they can't fly.

LEOLA. I can. I will. I mean that. I am not having anyone risk their life anymore to see me.

FRANK. Well, when the Russells come, driving, they'll be risking their lives. Especially with his eyes as bad as they are. And the Hudsons, driving. And the Harrison, driving ...

LEOLA. Well, they may as well skip the visit. It won't be the same. It'll be like trying to talk to Moses.

FRANK. Moses? Moses who?

LEOLA. In the Bible Moses. Suppose you ran into Moses on the street. What would you have to talk to him about? What? He doesn't know about radio or TV or movies or ...

FRANK. But we know about movies and radio and TV.

LEOLA. You missed my point.

FRANK. I don't think there was a point.

LEOLA. There was a point. Never mind.

FRANK. There are all sorts of people for you to get to know.

LEOLA. I'm too old to start over with new people. All that introducing yourself, telling them where you were born, and where you've lived. And what you've done and what you wish you had done.

FRANK. They'll love to hear that. That's how it's done.

LEOLA. It's boring. I've had a dull life.

FRANK. You've had an interesting life.

LEOLA. They couldn't make a movie out of it.

FRANK. So? Who do you know whose life has been better?

LEOLA. I'm not talking about better or worse. I'm talking about sitting across a table from a bunch of people who don't know any of the places I know. They won't know the names of my friends. I'll have to fill them in on everything. That's so boring when you're telling a story, stopping every few seconds to get all the facts straight for a one minute episode about the time Rose O'Laughlin at work poured Coca Cola on the snake plant. I'll bore them.

FRANK. They all have Rose O'Laughlin stories.

LEOLA. I won't want to hear theirs. If I didn't know Rose and Margaret in the steno pool and Sally in bookkeeping I wouldn't want to hear about when Rose poured Coca Cola on the snake plant and it grew three inches in two days.

FRANK. I thought it was funny.

LEOLA. No you didn't.

FRANK. I laughed.

LEOLA. No. That was not laughing what you did. This is what you did. Just like this. *(She makes a coughing, hacking sound.)* You coughed.

FRANK. I laughed. I remember laughing.

LEOLA. It was a cough. It sounded like you were clearing your throat.

FRANK. That's how I laugh.

LEOLA. You don't laugh like that.

FRANK. I do too. At times. That's just how I do it.

LEOLA. When you feel obligated to laugh but you don't want to but think you should, you make a hacking sound. It may fool some people, but not me. I've been around you a long time.

FRANK. I have different laughs. For different stories. I laugh different ways. But that was a laugh.

LEOLA. When you think a story is funny, like the ones George Copinski tells, like those you laugh like this. *(She laughs loudly and rolls around on her chair.)* That's how you do it when you think something is funny.

FRANK. Yes. I laugh like that for some things. For off color jokes I laugh like that. But the Coca Cola story which was quite amusing and which will amuse a lot of other people – well, anyone with plants and there are a lot of those kinds of people in Miami like that – for that kind of a story you don't roll on the floor. It's a quieter sort of laugh.

(He coughs out a laugh.)

LEOLA. That's just how you did it. Like you were taking your last breath. It sounded like you were choking and spitting up. I don't want to sit around with a bunch of strangers who sound like they're gagging when I tell them about myself.

FRANK. They won't. The Girardis are lovely people. Lovely. They had me in for coffee. They asked all about you.

LEOLA. We can move into an apartment around here. Westgate Village out by the highway! Very nice. Maureen Olson was there for a party and she just raved. And you know Maureen is not easily impressed.

FRANK. I'm not staying here. I went down to Miami, picked out a lovely condominium, three swimming pools, twelve laundry facilities, a supermarket two blocks away, I've written to Social Security already so they can send my checks to my new bank. We're moving. Drink your coffee.

LEOLA. You won't even drive by Westgate Village?

FRANK. It's not on the way to Miami.

LEOLA. Well then you have to promise me a few things.

FRANK. Like what?

LEOLA. Like I want you to ... quit cigarettes. In that little, dinky condominium ...

FRANK. It is not little. It is not dinky. You saw the floor plan.

LEOLA. With the windows sealed shut it'll smell awful the way you smoke around the clock.

FRANK. I've tried to give it up. You know what happens. I get those blisters on my lips.

LEOLA. I'm not going if you keep smoking. It's not fair to my lungs.

FRANK. Okay. I'll go to one of those clinics they have where they help you stop smoking. No, better yet, I'll get one of those patch things they're advertising all the time on the TV.

LEOLA. And since there will be a swimming pool handy ...

FRANK. Not two hundred feet away. Very clean. I didn't even see any bugs in it.

LEOLA. I will want to swim.

FRANK. Good.

LEOLA. Which means I'll need to go to the hairdressers every day.

FRANK. For what?

LEOLA. My hair. I'm not wearing a cap in the pool. That doesn't save your hair anyway. It smashes the curl right out of it. I'll need to get it done every day. Maybe twice a day. Depending.

FRANK. On what?

LEOLA. If I go in twice a day. In the morning and maybe later in the afternoon.

FRANK. That's fifteen, twenty dollars a throw.

LEOLA. I can't do it myself. I can roll it up fine. But combing it out always defeats me. It'll look so bad it won't matter how good a job I did rolling it up. If we stayed here Margie Talbot could comb me out.

FRANK. Okay. You can get your hair done. If you go in that often I'm sure they can give you a better price.

LEOLA. I want new furniture.

FRANK. Ours is already to go with the movers. This furniture is fine.

LEOLA. Not in a brand new condominium. With freshly painted walls. And with all new carpets. We'll need new.

FRANK. The truck is coming for this.

LEOLA. We can get rid of it down there. Maybe we can get a deal on it at the furniture place we go to.

FRANK. That green chair is only a year old.

LEOLA. Next to brand new it'll look fifteen or twenty. We're so well heeled. You're always saying so. So we'll get new furniture.

FRANK. Well heeled yes because I haven't been foolish with our money.

LEOLA. If you don't want to spend it on our apartment, I don't know what you will spend it on.

FRANK. Your hair.

LEOLA. That's only because I care how I look. Don't you want me to look nice? Don't you want that condominium to look nice? It costs money.

FRANK. Well maybe we should replace some of it.

LEOLA. All of it. I want to go Oriental.

FRANK. Orien*tal? (He thinks better of protesting further. Then, pleasantly.)* That will be very nice in that apartment with the celery green walls.

LEOLA. I want a maid. I want a cook. I'm sick of cleaning. I'm sick of cooking. And I want a chauffeur. Frankly anymore in the car with you I don't feel safe.

FRANK. Is that all?

LEOLA. Hair. Maid. Cook. Did I say cook?

FRANK. Yes.

LEOLA. I'm sick of cooking. Chauffeur.

FRANK. Furniture. Don't leave out furniture.

LEOLA. It'll look shabby. Cleaning lady. That's all.

FRANK. *(Pause)* We're going to Miami. No cook. No maid. No chauffeur. I'm going to smoke. No new furniture.

LEOLA. Well then cancel the truck.

FRANK. Get dressed. Get your clothes on.

LEOLA. I don't want to go.

FRANK. Strip your bed. Put your sheets in the box.

LEOLA. I don't want to move.

FRANK. Get your clothes on and put your nightgown in your suitcase. *(LEOLA starts looking through the boxes.)* What are you looking for now? *(LEOLA gets out a pot and finds a package of noodles.)* What are you doing?

LEOLA. Making some noodles.

FRANK. Now?

LEOLA. I'm hungry for some buttered noodles. I'm upset, I get hungry.

FRANK. Have a piece of toast.

LEOLA. I am long past the point where a piece of toast will comfort me.

FRANK. You can't be cooking with the movers coming.

LEOLA. Why not? They're not taking the stove. What about that?

FRANK. What about what?

LEOLA. Maybe we should take the stove.

FRANK. We have a stove in the apartment. Now go strip your bed.

LEOLA. But not this stove. So many memories. I taught the kids how to cook on this stove. All of them. Gloria. And Joanna. And Jimmy. I think it's a mistake to leave this. You pack up, and leave all your memories behind.

FRANK. We'll make new memories.

LEOLA. What's wrong with the old ones?

FRANK. We'll add them to the new ones.

LEOLA. I stood right here with Jimmy, right on this spot, taught him how to make a tuna casserole ...

FRANK. Don't start on Jimmy now.

LEOLA. Who's starting? I'm remembering. What else do we have to do? Everything's packed.

FRANK. Almost everything.

(She puts the pot back into the box and shuts the lid.)

LEOLA. See how fast I can be packed? *(She returns to the stove.)* I stood right here. I think this is even the very spot. I think it is. I got the casserole I used in there someplace.

FRANK. Don't look for it now. This is not show and tell.

LEOLA. Visual aids come in handy. Like the stove. I stood right here.

FRANK. Maybe you want to take some of the floor.

LEOLA. I won't even dignify that. I stood right here. I told Jimmy how to grease the bowl, and then sprinkle it with bread crumbs to be the lining ...

FRANK. What the hell are you going on about Jimmy for now? You didn't even want to go to his memorial.

LEOLA. If we go to Florida, there won't be anything there of Jimmy. Nothing. He'll be all gone. Here he's still with us. Every place I look. He's still here.

FRANK. *(Carefully)* No he isn't Leola.

LEOLA. I know he isn't. I'm not getting loony. But, it's only like he's out, gone out, someplace, not dead. I can think he's going to call me only he got too busy with stuff so maybe tomorrow, or over the weekend.

FRANK. He isn't going to call.

LEOLA. I know that.

FRANK. Sometimes I don't think you do. Really.

LEOLA. Do *you?*

FRANK. Every day.

LEOLA. So you're well adjusted.

FRANK. If you'd let yourself go at the memorial service. That's what they're for ...

LEOLA. Oh that memorial service. What was that?

FRANK. Well it was a lot more fitting than what you had in mind.

LEOLA. Fitting is as fitting does.

FRANK. Going to see some Barbra Streisand movie is no kind of fitting tribute.

LEOLA. Jimmy liked Barbra Streisand. He had all her records. And we went to see that first movie of hers, *Funny Girl,* and then later *Funny Lady.* And we saw *The Way We Were* on the TV once when he was visiting. So it would have been fitting.

FRANK. Well, you may as well have not been there. You hardly cried at all.

LEOLA. Yeah. I know. I was surprised too. I thought I would. That wasn't ever how I saw myself being when I used to think about it. Dry eyed.

FRANK. Think about it? You used to think about that?

LEOLA. I'd pretend to myself sometimes. I'd see people on TV being told some terrible thing, about someone they loved, and I'd think if anyone ever came here and told me that Jimmy was dead, how terrible that would be and I'd get so teary eyed just thinking about it, I'd go to pieces. Just thinking about it. And then I didn't when it did really happen. Maybe it got all used up when I was practicing.

FRANK. You'd pretend something like that?

LEOLA. Every now and then. If I was watching something like that on the news. It's only normal.

FRANK. Normal? You call that normal? Crying when he isn't dead. And not crying when he is dead.

LEOLA. I'm sorry I wasn't a fountain of tears. But that's how I reacted.

FRANK. Well, I hope by the time I go – if I go first – your reactions are just a bit more in line with the rest of the world's. I don't want you sitting on your rear end in some movie theatre with me laid out some place and all our friends are wondering where in hell you are.

LEOLA. I wouldn't do that for you.

FRANK. Good. I can die in peace.

LEOLA. You don't like movies. There'd be no point.

FRANK. It was right that I took you to the church. That was the proper place I don't care what you say.

LEOLA. What's a church? I ask you that. What, when you think about it, what is a church?

FRANK. It's the place where his friends came from all over to organize a memorial tribute, a real one.

LEOLA. I wanted to do my own memorial my own way.

FRANK. Seeing some Barbra Streisand movie with your son not even five days dead was no kind of tribute anybody could understand.

LEOLA. Well that thing they staged wasn't so hot. What kind of memorial was that anyway? No body. No body to look at. Just some damn empty box that the funeral people would rent out again for another five hundred bucks. And don't think they don't. What kind of a memorial was that?

FRANK. The best they could do.

LEOLA. You were all so convinced he was dead.

FRANK. He was dead.

LEOLA. You got proof? He could be out there still. An amnesiac. And when you least expect it, boom, there he is knocking at the door, and we won't be here. We'll be in Florida. Only he won't know that.

FRANK. He isn't going to come knocking on the door. The plane blew up.

LEOLA. So they said.

FRANK. All the people blew up. 30,000 feet. He's dead. Don't you think?

LEOLA. He didn't need to die. If he'd stayed closer he wouldn't have been on that plane.

FRANK. You know why he lived far away.

LEOLA. *(With contempt.)* Yeah, yeah. His job. His life. His goals. His ambitions. So what?

FRANK. We wanted him to have ambitions.

LEOLA. I never should have sent him to those art classes when he was little. You were right, always pushing the sports at him. I should have let you have your way more, instead of all the time saying let him be interested in what he's interested in. I led him straight to his grave. I was a bad mother doing what I did. Those art classes lead to his death.

FRANK. No, no. You were a good mother. You know you were a good mother.

LEOLA. Yeah? Was I?

FRANK. He could have been a pro ball player and been on planes all the time.

LEOLA. Him? What kind of ball player could he have been? He was never on any teams.

FRANK. Okay, all right. A ... lawyer. A lawyer. He could have been a lawyer. Flying all over defending people, being on planes all the time.

LEOLA. A lawyer? Not with his gifts. He was gifted. They said so. In the 6th grade. "Your son is gifted." It wasn't just me who thought that.

FRANK. I'm only saying.

LEOLA. I know what you're saying. I killed him. Say it. You think it, say it. Don't hint. Say it. I killed him.

FRANK. You didn't kill him. I'm only talking possibilities.

LEOLA. We must have done something he didn't like.

FRANK. Nothing I know about. Nothing he ever said anything about.

LEOLA. Then why'd he leave us? Why didn't he stay here where people loved him?

FRANK. He grew up.

LEOLA. Why'd he have to grow up? Why didn't he stay little? It was like he abducted himself; kidnapped himself away from us. Took himself away. Held himself hostage. I wasn't done yet. I wasn't through with him yet.

FRANK. I wasn't either.

LEOLA. I can shut my eyes – I don't even have to shut them – I can see him clear, standing in his choir robe, the one he had when we were going to the Methodist church, and I took his picture in it for our Christmas card. And all the other times. I thought it was good having a memory. I hate my memory. You should not die before your parents. You put your parents through so much anyway. At least they should not have to be around when you die. There should be a law.

FRANK. A law?

LEOLA. A law of nature. A cosmic law. You should not see what you brought into this world go out of it. It is not a nice thing. *(Crying)* Nothing. Nothing. We've got nothing. *(FRANK goes to comfort her. She pulls away from him.)* Not anything. Not one more look.

FRANK. Like you said. Over there. I see him getting the car keys. And there, putting change left over from getting the milk and bread. And there, watching TV. And there, standing at the refrigerator. I see him a hundred times a day. *(He turns to her.)* You think he was only yours! I got the news too! They told me too! We lost our boy. We did. Not just you. We did.

(She goes to him. She puts her hands on either side of his face.)

LEOLA. Yes. Yes we did. We did. *(LEOLA puts her arms around him. He then puts his arms around her. In a moment she pulls away from him and returns to the table. She looks at Jimmy's plate. She picks it up. She turns to FRANK and holds Jimmy's plate out to him. He takes it and holds it. She picks up the carton for the dishes and puts it on the table. She folds back the flaps and steps back. FRANK steps forward and carefully puts Jimmy's plate in the box. LEOLA joins him and they join hands, looking at the plate in the box. In a moment they separate and begin silently packing the remaining dishes. In a bit, as they continue to pack, they resume speaking.)* You aren't afraid of how it'll be just you and me?

FRANK. Afraid of what?

LEOLA. Being alone.

FRANK. We've been alone before.

LEOLA. No. Never.

FRANK. Sure we have. Before the kids. After the kids.

LEOLA. Never. There's always been somebody to go to. Your parents. Mine. The kids. Your friends. My friends. Our friends. Now we're going to Miami where we won't know anybody. We'll be all alone. Together. In that apartment. Not even a backyard.

FRANK. We have a patio.

LEOLA. That's not what I mean. You missed my point.

FRANK. I did not. You're afraid we'll get there, we find out we don't have anything in common except for the years we spent together.

LEOLA. Aren't you? How often can we sit down and kick around 1959? Or Christmas 1967?

FRANK. We'll have new experiences.

LEOLA. Like finding out we don't have anything in common.

FRANK. We have a lot in common.

LEOLA. I needlepoint. You drink beer. I go to the library. You sleep on the couch.

FRANK. So I'll go to the library. I'll learn to sew. And you can sleep on the couch. *(She makes a face. He takes the packed carton of dishes and sets it on the floor with the other cartons.)* You want us to have mutual activities. So do I. We have that in common. That's what got us here in the first place. I saw you at that dance in 1951 at the Aztec Ballroom on Montgomery. It was a Saturday. September the 15th. You had on a red dress.

LEOLA. My mother made it for me.

FRANK. You were lovely.

LEOLA. She made one in blue for my sister.

FRANK. It looked better in red. I said to David Morrison. I said, "See that girl? I want to have mutual activities in common with her." I wanted us to be alone together. But it's been like being at a dance being married to you. Someone always cutting in. But we always had the last dance together. Always. Didn't we?

LEOLA. Yes. You always told whoever barged in that the last dance was taken.

FRANK. I saw to it then and I'm seeing to it now. I want to be alone with you. If I didn't I'd have said, "Let's get an apartment around here. Let's stay close to friends. I don't want to be alone with you." But I didn't say that. Did I?

LEOLA. No. You said let's go to Miami.

FRANK. So I can finally have you all alone to myself. No more cutting in. I don't even want to share you with pots and pans.

LEOLA. You're going to wish I had a sinkfull of dishes. You're going to be so bored.

FRANK. I know how it's going to be. It's going to be like it was when we first met. We enjoyed that.

LEOLA. Yes. We did.

FRANK. I had to wait a long time back there in 1951 to get a dance with you. But it was worth it.

LEOLA. I remember when you put your hand on my back I thought, "Oh this is going to be a good dance. He knows how to lead." Some of those guys just couldn't. Larry Newman. He was lousy. I'd dance with him and it felt like I was dancing with a bulldozer. You knew how to lead though. I knew it the second we started. *(She offers him her hand and they begin dancing. He is humming/singing.)* Did I ever tell you the story about the time when Rose O'Laughlin poured Coca Cola on the snake plant on her desk and -- honest to God, no lie -- it grew 3 inches in 2 days. *(He laughs uproaringly. She looks at him like he's nuts.)* That story isn't that funny. You never laugh right.

(They continue dancing and laughing as the lights fade.)

THE END

PROPERTY PLOT

1 table large enough to seat six
5 chairs for the table
1 tablecloth for the table
5 dinner plates
5 salad plates
5 dessert plates
2 coffee cups and saucers
2 coffee mugs
1 pot with lid
Bubblewrap and newspapers
Packing cartons for the dishes, tablecloth, pot and lid
    (at least six cartons – various sizes)

COSTUME PLOT

FRANK:
    Casual pants; loafers or sneakers; brightly colored short sleeve shirt ala Hawaiian style.

LEOLA:
    Slippers or casual slip ons; earrings; caftan with zipper or button front (not a bathrobe).

FLOOR PLAN

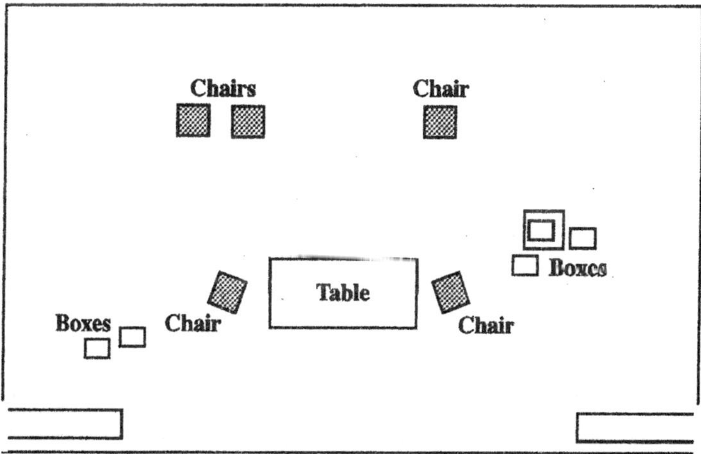

HARRIET TUBMAN VISITS A THERAPIST

by

Carolyn Gage

"She declares that before her escape from slavery, she used to dream of flying over fields and towns, and rivers and mountains, looking down upon them 'like a bird,' and reaching at last a great fence or sometimes a river, over which she would try to fly, 'but it 'peared like I wouldn't hab de strength, and jes as I was sinkin' down, dere would be ladies all drest in white ober dere, and dey would put out dere arms and pull me 'cross.'"

– from an article about Harriet Tubman
in *The Boston Commonwealth*, 1863.

HARRIET TUBMAN VISITS A THERAPIST
by
Carolyn Gage

with

THE THERAPIST . . . . Deana J. Becker

HARRIET TUBMAN . . . . Emmanuela Souffrant

Directed by Jennifer Spence

Produced by
Love Creek Productions, New York City

ABOUT THE AUTHOR

CAROLYN GAGE is a lesbian-feminist playwright, author, and activist. Her collection of plays *The Second Coming of Joan of Arc and Other Plays* (HerBooks 1994) was named a national finalist for the Lambda Literary Awards, and she has written the first lesbian theatre manual, *Take Stage! How to Direct and Produce a Lesbian Play* (Scarecrow Press, 1997) and the first book of scenes and monologues for lesbian actors (Odd Girls Press, 1999). Her complete catalog of work can be found online at <http://www.javanet.com/~cgage>.

CHARACTERS

HARRIET TUBMAN: An African American woman, mid-twenties.
THE THERAPIST: An African American woman.

SETTING

Place: Interior of a therapist's office.
Time: Another dimension of space-time.

(Setting: A contemporary therapist's office with pictures of peaceful landscapes and recovery literature in the bookcase. There is a desk, but the THERAPIST has done much to create a non-threatening, informal atmosphere.)

(At Rise: The THERAPIST is reviewing HARRIET's file. She is a light-skinned African American woman who wears the clothing of a contemporary middle-class therapist. There is a soft knock on the door. The THERAPIST closes the file and rises.)

THERAPIST. Come in. *(There is another knock, and she crosses to the door and opens it. HARRIET TUBMAN stands in the doorway. HARRIET is a dark-skinned African American woman, about 27, wearing the clothing of an enslaved field worker. HARRIET's speech and movements are deliberately slow and dull at first. She stands waiting for orders, head bowed.)* Come in. Harriet Tubman? You're right on time. *(She gestures into the room. HARRIET lifts her eyes briefly. Her face is expressionless.)* Please ... Either chair. Make yourself comfortable. *(HARRIET shuffles towards one of the chairs and sits. She keeps her head down. The THERAPIST sits in her chair. There is a long silence. The THERAPIST sighs and smiles at HARRIET.)* I understand that you have spells of narcolepsy ... *(No response.)* You have brief periodic spells of deep sleep? *(HARRIET nods briefly, eyes down.)* And they can come on any time – when you're working? *(HARRIET nods again.)* Ever since you were a girl, wasn't it? *(HARRIET glances at her quickly, then down again.)* I understand that's when these spells came on – when you were a girl ...

HARRIET. Dey come on when de man thow'd de chunk o'lead in mah face.

THERAPIST. And you were a girl then?

HARRIET. Not aftuh dat.

THERAPIST. How do you feel about that? *(HARRIET lowers her eyes again.)* I would feel pretty angry if someone threw a lead weight at me. *(HARRIET remains motionless. The THERAPIST changes her tone.)* Harriet, do you know why you're here?

HARRIET. Massuh Edward done sent me.

THERAPIST. Do you know why?

HARRIET. Cain't sell no nigga like me.

THERAPIST. I don't think that's why. *(HARRIET looks down.)* I understand why you feel that way. That's a very natural conclusion for a slave to draw. But in this case, I think Mr. Brodas is genuinely concerned about you, and I have reasons for why I say that. Do you want to hear them? *(No response.)* I think Mr. Brodas likes you. He speaks about you with a great deal of pride. He's allowed you to choose your own husband, and John Tubman is a free man. That's a very unusual thing for a slaveowner to do. And he lets you hire out to a shipbuilder –

HARRIET. He take alluh money.

THERAPIST. Well, that's not exactly true. I understand that you get to keep what you make over what you owe him. *(HARRIET snorts.)* I understand you've been able to buy yourself a pair of oxen. That's pretty impressive. *(No response.)* You could even buy your freedom someday.

HARRIET. Time I'ze daid.

THERAPIST. *(The THERAPIST studies HARRIET for a moment.)* You know I share your feelings about slavery. All day long I listen to women tell me stories that make me sick. Stories of rape – raping children, of beating – beating pregnant women, stories of murder, or torture, of live burnings, of babies being sold away from their mothers, of chain gangs ... *(HARRIET looks away.)* But I'm not going to change it, and neither are you. We can drive ourselves crazy thinking about it. We can kill ourselves fighting it. Or we can make the most of what is possible. Like you did, buying your oxen.

HARRIET. *(Eyes down.)* Nat Turner.

THERAPIST. What?

HARRIET. *(Looking at the THERAPIST for the first time as she speaks. HARRIET drops the dull-witted act.)* Nat Turner. He killed fifty-seven whitefolks.

THERAPIST. *(Taken aback by HARRIET's intensity.)* They hanged Nat Turner.

HARRIET. *(Looking at her hands, acting again.)* Hanged a man las' week over to Bucktown for stealin' chickens.

THERAPIST. *(Losing her temper.)* Nat Turner is the reason you can't read. Did you know that? After his uprising, they made it illegal to teach slaves to read or write. After Nat Turner, we couldn't even meet to go to church, unless a whiteman was the preacher. After Nat Turner, they wouldn't let us talk to each other in the fields, but they wouldn't let us just work either. Oh, no. After Nat Turner, we all had to sing while we worked – oh, except of course, "Go Down, Moses." Now, thanks to Nat Turner, you can die for singing that song.

HARRIET. *(Singing)*
O GO DOWN, MOSES,
WAY DOWN IN EGYPT'S LAND ...

THERAPIST. You think I'm an uncle tom, don't you?

HARRIET. *(Continues singing.)*
TELL OLE PHARAOH,
LET MY PEOPLE GO ...

THERAPIST. You think I sold out.

HARRIET. *(Closing her eyes, she raises her voice.)*
OLE PHARAOH SAID HE WOULD GO CROSS.
O GO DOWN, MOSES.

LET MY PEOPLE GO.
AND DON'T GET LOST IN THE WILDERNESS.
LET MY PEOPLE GO.
(HARRIET looks at the THERAPIST, who is silent now.) Didn't hab no gun.
THERAPIST. Who didn't have a gun?
HARRIET. Prophet Turner. A sword. Can you see dat? Had hissef a sword! *(She laughs.)* What he gonna do wid a sword? Slit open de sow's belly?
THERAPIST. Are you thinking of killing someone?
HARRIET. *(Looking at her hands.)* Mebbe I buy a mule to go 'long wid de ox.
THERAPIST. *(Sizing her up.)* I'm going to be frank with you. Mr. Brodas has sent you to me, because he's afraid you're going to run away.
HARRIET. *(Bursts out laughing.)* Oh, he skeered!
THERAPIST. *(Pleasantly)* Well, that's why you're here, and I'm afraid I have to agree with his observation.
HARRIET. *(Enjoying the idea.)* He tell you dat Harriet bin lookin' mighty greazy.

(She laughs.)

THERAPIST. "Greazy?"
HARRIET. Gonna slip hersef th'oo de massuh's han's.

(She laughs again.)

THERAPIST. *(Smiling along with the joke.)* Your husband seems to think you've been "lookin' mighty greazy," too.
HARRIET. *(She stops laughing.)* John say dat? He tell you dat?
THERAPIST. He told Mr. Brodas. *(HARRIET is stunned.)* Harriet, nobody's against you here. Your husband loves you and Mr. Brodas has a great deal of respect for you. But, if you run away, neither one of them is going to be able to save you from the slave catchers – or their dogs. You've got too much to live for to throw your life away like that.
HARRIET. John bin talkin' to Massuh Edward?
THERAPIST. *(Rising)* Harriet, I want to help you. You are in a very serious situation. Mr. Brodas has asked me to determine whether or not I think you're going to run. *(HARRIET looks at her.)* I'm going to tell him that I'd like to see you for a few more visits, but after that, unless there's a change in your attitude, I will have to tell him the truth. I doubt he'll let you hire out after that. *(HARRIET says nothing. The THERAPIST turns suddenly.)* Look at you! You're young, you're healthy, you're in love, you work for wages, your husband is a free man – That's a lot to be thankful for! You have less reason to run than most. *(HARRIET remains silent.)* And what about your family – your mother? She was the one who saved your

life when you got the head injury, wasn't she? She was right there with you, wasn't she? Are you going to abandon her? You know you'll never see her again. *(HARRIET looks down.)* And what about John? He's a good man, Harriet. You're pushing away the people who love you in the name of freedom. You're so busy dreaming about a world you don't have, you're missing out on the one right here. Learn to focus on the things you *can* change, learn to appreciate what you have right now – and you can be a great force for good. Little by little, one day at a time, your life will get better and better. *(HARRIET says nothing. The THERAPIST sits at her desk and looks out the window.)* I knew a woman once who decided to run. You could say she'd been "lookin' mighty greazy." One night, she took her two daughters – one was six and the other twelve – and she ran. *(HARRIET is keenly interested. The THERAPIST turns back to her.)* They caught her, of course, as they catch most runaways.

HARRIET. How far she git?

THERAPIST. To the Delaware border. *(HARRIET nods. The THERAPIST narrates the rest of her story with clinical detachment.)* It was the hounds that got her. By the time they called off the dogs, her daughter – the six-year old – was already dead. And then they took turns raping the twelve-year old while they made the mother watch. After that, she wouldn't have anything to do with the child. She wouldn't touch her, wouldn't talk to her. She treated her like she didn't exist. Right up until the girl was sold down South. *(HARRIET says nothing.)* Do you think this woman made a wise decision?

HARRIET. She didn't hab no gun?

THERAPIST. What if she did? She was outnumbered. Or do you think she should have shot her daughters?

HARRIET. *(Shrugging)* Lib in de no'th or die in de south.

THERAPIST. You would shoot your own children?

HARRIET. I seen mah sistuhs – Linah and Soph – seen 'em sol' off on de chain gang, an' dat day I wisht dey wuz daid, an' I bin prayin' dey was daid ev'y day aftuh dat, too.

THERAPIST. Enough to kill them?

HARRIET. Ain't no livin' when dey kin do yo' body any way dey like.

THERAPIST. *(Vehement)* Oh, yes, there is! We are so much more than our physical bodies –

HARRIET. *(Cutting her off, she rises.)* Look! Now, you look! *(She pulls her shirt out and pulls up the back.)* Heah – you look at dat. You look at what de whiteman done.

THERAPIST. *(Turning away.)* I've seen plenty of scars.

HARRIET. No, you look, cuz you ain't seen dis 'oman's scars. You therapizin' on me, you look. You stan' up heah, an' you look. *(The THERAPIST looks.)* You see dat? Dat is a fiel' o' flesh been ploughed by de debil's own han'.

THERAPIST. But you *don't* have to let it scar your soul.

HARRIET. What you talkin' 'bout? Mah soul? Dis heah is mah soul! Dis black Ashanti skin is mah soul!

(She turns to face the THERAPIST.)

THERAPIST. *(Becoming very clinical.)* And what does it do for you to keep remembering?

HARRIET. *(HARRIET starts to respond with anger, but she stops herself. A smile spreads slowly over her face.)* You is sleepin' wid de massuh.

THERAPIST. *(Hesitating, she chooses her words carefully.)* Sometimes Mr. Brodas visits with me. *(HARRIET is still smiling.)* That doesn't affect my belief that your running away would be suicidal.

HARRIET. *(Lowering her head.)* Yas'm.

THERAPIST. And it doesn't affect the fact that I want to help you.

HARRIET. *(Mumbling)* No'm.

THERAPIST. You don't have to put on an act for me. *(HARRIET looks up, puzzled.)* I know what you're doing. *(Silence)* You don't have to please me.

HARRIET. *(Eager to please.)* If you doan' want me to be pleasin, den I won't. No ma'am. Sartainly I won't. You des see how pleasin', Harriet kin be. I kin be de downright unpleasin'est –

THERAPIST. *(Cutting her off.)* Stop it!

HARRIET. Yas'm.

(The two women sit in silence.)

THERAPIST. *(Starting over.)* I sleep with Mr. Brodas ... *(Hesitating)* He's a kind man.

HARRIET. Oh, yas'm, dat he is. He be de bes' massuh in de world! Dat's des what I allus say, dat Massuh Edward, he –

THERAPIST. *(Cutting her off.)* I hate him. *(HARRIET watches her.)* I hate him, because he's white, because he's a slaveowner, because he's a drunkard, because he's a coward and a liar, I hate him because he uses women, I hate him because he doesn't bother to wash when he comes to me. I hate him so much, believe it or not, he doesn't bother me. I hate him so much, I don't let him have anything.

HARRIET. He got yo' body.

THERAPIST. I'm not in it. *(HARRIET says nothing.)* I haven't been in it since I was twelve and I watched the dogs tear my little sister to pieces. I had already left my body before the first whiteman climbed on top of me. And I wasn't in my body when they raped my mother. I wasn't in my body when they sold me down south. And I wasn't in my body when I had a whiteman's baby at thirteen. I wasn't in my body when they sold her five years later. And I wasn't in my body when Mr. Brodas made his proposition. But, you show me your skin, Harriet – let me show you my soul. It's here ... *(She takes out a locket.)* This is my daughter, Felicity. She lives with me. She has never had to work in the fields, and she never will, because I am buying her freedom. This, this is my soul. I keep myself alive for her ...

HARRIET. While you is larnin' de other women to be de slaves.

THERAPIST. I teach them how to survive. Look – these are my files. Here are the stories of women who've come to me. Women who didn't go crazy, who didn't kill themselves. Women I *helped*. And I have helped women, Harriet. Maybe not you. But I have helped women. *(She pauses. HARRIET says nothing.)* I give them a safe place to express themselves – to let out their grief and their rage. I help them speak the unspeakable. I listen. I validate their suffering. I teach them strategies for surviving – *(She breaks off.)* You think this is bullshit. *(HARRIET says nothing.)* How many women could live day to day with your level of rage? You don't have children. What do you think that anger would do to a child? And how long do you think you're going to be able to live like this? Oh, you can make a run for it, all right. But Pennsylvania is a long way off. Do you really think you're going to have the stamina to make it? It takes a cool head to go the distance, and I can tell you right now, Harriet Tubman, you don't have it. Your rage will get you over the county line, maybe. But the Delaware border? Unh-unh. Never.

HARRIET. *(The THERAPIST has hit a nerve, and HARRIET reconsiders.)* So when you work wid de women ...

THERAPIST. I teach stress management ... relaxation techniques. Visualization. Sometimes I do a guided meditation with women.

HARRIET. An' dat is what?

THERAPIST. That is where I put the client under hypnosis – which is like your sleeping spells – and then I talk them through an experience they're afraid of – like a whipping, or an auction where their children are going to be sold ... or I prepare them if they have to submit sexually to their owner. *(She pauses.)* I give them images – I teach them to go away ... so they can bear it.

HARRIET. An' dis keep de women goin'?

THERAPIST. Yes. Yes, it does. They learn that reality is only another state of consciousness, and it gives them some control. Otherwise, of course, they have none.

HARRIET. *(Making up her mind.)* You bin up no'th.

THERAPIST. I was captured.

HARRIET. You bin to Delaware.

THERAPIST. To the border.

HARRIET. Draw me dat map.

THERAPIST. I can't do that. *(HARRIET looks at her.)* I don't encourage my clients to take reckless chances with their lives.

HARRIET. *(Angry, she rises.)* I got two rights – de right to freedom and de right to die.

THERAPIST. *(The THERAPIST rises.)* I have the right to live.

HARRIET. Libbin'! What you talkin', 'oman? You ain't eben inside yo' own skin!

(HARRIET, enraged, turns to go. She opens the door, but is seized by a fit of narcolepsy. The THERAPIST helps her to a chair. She watches HARRIET for a moment, and then she closes the door.)

THERAPIST. You want the map? All right, Harriet Tubman, I'll give you the map ... Oh, I'll give you the map. *(She pulls a chair close to the "sleeping" HARRIET.)* Harriet, listen to me. We don't have very much time, and I want you to listen and remember. You are standing in the middle of a field. It's the field behind the Brodas plantation. It's night time, Harriet, and you are alone. You are standing in the field, and you are looking back towards the cabins. Can you see them? *(HARRIET doesn't move.)* It's dark, and everyone is asleep, Harriet, everyone except you. You are wide awake, standing in the field. You turn back towards the cabins – and there's your cabin – can you see it? Nod your head if you can see it. *(HARRIET still doesn't move, and the THERAPIST discovers the cause of her resistance.)* Harriet, listen to me. You are having to go alone. You are leaving tonight. John is asleep in the cabin. You are leaving without him. Can you see the cabin where John Tubman is sleeping? *(Slowly, HARRIET nods.)* It's a clear night and the stars are out. Look up, and see if you can see one star that's brighter than the others, the one in the "drinking gourd." It should be right over the cabins. Do you see it? *(HARRIET nods.)* Good. That's the North Star. You're going to keep that in front of this shoulder. *(She taps HARRIET's left shoulder.)* This shoulder. Now remember that. It's a warm night, Harriet, and you're not afraid. Lift up your arms. Lift them up. *(HARRIET lifts her arms slightly.)* Are you ready? *(HARRIET nods.)* Take a deep breath, and as you breathe in, feel yourself becoming lighter. Breathe in again. You are becoming lighter and lighter, lighter than a feather. Lighter than the smoke of a candle flame. Keep breathing in. You are rising in the warm air. Feel yourself rising. Your toes are just barely touching the ground ... just barely, and now they're not touching at all. You are rising like smoke, up over the field. Higher and higher. Look down, Harriet, and see the cabins. They're just little boxes under you, as you rise higher and higher, keeping that North Star over this shoulder. *(She touches her again.)* And now you're over the big house ... You're flying over the edge of the fields now, over Greenbrier Swamp. You can see the black water shining through the trees with the reflection of the moon. And you stay on the edge of the swamp, Harriet. Can you see it? *(She nods.)* And now the swamp is opening up, widening. And you're over the Choptank River. The Choptank River is right under you. And you're flying faster now, because you need to keep going, over the Choptank, and it's getting smaller and smaller. Follow the Choptank, Harriet, about seventy miles on the Choptank River. And see where you are now? See the river, how small it is? It's just a stream now, isn't it? *(HARRIET nods.)* You're very close to the Delaware border now. Very close. There's a farm on the other side of the border, the Cowgill farm in Willow Grove, and that's all you need to know, because once you get to the Cowgill farm, they'll take care of you the rest of the way into Pennsylvania. All you have to do is get to the farm. You understand? *(HARRIET nods.)* So you're going to go down now. Down through the trees, down into Delaware. You're almost on the ground now, almost touching the ground ... Listen! Listen, Harriet! Hear that? What is it? Listen! *(HARRIET stiffens.)* It's dogs barking, isn't it? Hear them? It's the dogs, Harriet! The dogs! They're after you. You can hear them coming. And you start to run, Harriet. *(HARRIET's breathing accelerates.)* Run! Run! And you're running, but it's night, and you can't see very well. You're tripping over the tree roots and the branches, and the dogs are getting louder and louder. *(HARRIET begins to breathe heavily.)* And now you can hear the men shouting! Listen! They've fired a shot! They hear the dogs, Harriet, and they're after you, and there's nowhere to hide. They're coming. And you're running so fast you can't breathe, and your heart is pounding so hard in your chest it hurts. And now you turn around, and you can see them, Harriet. You can see the dogs coming for you. And you know what they're going to do. You've seen them catching possums and squirrels. And you know what they're going to do to you. And you're trying to run, but you trip. You're on the ground, Harriet, and you can't get up. And now, I'm going to count backwards from five –

HARRIET. *(Breaking through with great effort, but still in a trance.)* I see dem! I see dem!

THERAPIST. You see the dogs?

HARRIET. I see de women.

THERAPIST. What women?

HARRIET. De women wid de lights. I see dem in de trees aroun' me. I see dem stretchin' out dey han's to me. Dey is callin' my name, an' I am reachin' out my han's to dem.

THERAPIST. There aren't any women with you. You are alone.

HARRIET. No, dat I ain't. I has got de company of so many women, dat I cain't see dem stars no mo' for de brightness of de women dat is 'roun me in dem trees. And dey is callin' out my name, say "Araminta" – dat what dey callin' me – "Araminta" – like my mamma. Dey is shinin' wid glory, dese black women, an' dey is reachin' out dey han's to me, gonna pull me up offa dat groun', gonna snatch me right 'way fum de mouf dem dogs and de han's of de whiteman. Gonna pull me on ober dat line. Doan matter I cain't walk, doan' matter I cain't run, doan matter I forget de way – doan matter, 'cuz dese women, dey been heah befo' and dey gonna bring me on acrost. Dey is shinin' an' laughin' an' dey is takin' me by de han' to freedom.

THERAPIST. Are you dying, Harriet?

HARRIET. *(Laughing in her trance.)* No, ma'am! Not befo' I live to see de lights of Phil'delphia!

THERAPIST. Harriet, these women don't exist.

HARRIET. Oh, yes, dey do. Dese is de women dat lib so good dey cain't die. Dese is de women fum Africa, de women who pitch deysefs off de ship, rather die dan lib in de chains ob slavery. Dese is de women who kilt dey own chilrun 'fo' dey see dem sol' on de auction block ... de women who kilt dey massuhs wid de ax, wid de hoe, wid dey bare han's, de women dey cain't skeer no mo' cause dey already done do de wors' an' dey still alibe. Dese is de women larnin' each other de ways to keep out de whiteman's babies befo' dey start growin' in de womb ob de black woman's body ... de women wid de spells make de whitefolks sick. Dese is de African women, de Ashanti women.

THERAPIST. *(Quietly)* I can't see those women.

(Smiling in her trance, HARRIET begins to sing, and the THERAPIST talks over her singing.)

HARRIET.
O GO DOWN, MOSES,
WAY DOWN IN EGYPT'S LAND
TELL OLE PHARAOH
LET MY PEOPLE GO.

THERAPIST.
Harriet, I'm going to count backwards from five. And when I say "one," you will open your eyes. You will be relaxed and fully alert. You will not remember any of this experience. Five ... four ... three ... two ... ONE.

(HARRIET opens her eyes, and the two women look at each other. The THERAPIST smiles.)

THERAPIST. How do you feel?

HARRIET. *(After a long pause.)* You sic de dogs on me.

THERAPIST. *(Pretending not to understand.)* I'm sorry?

HARRIET. You sic de dogs on me. De whiteman's dogs.

THERAPIST. I don't know what you're talking about.

HARRIET. De dogs in yo' haid. You ain't buyin' no freedom fo' nobody wid dem dogs in yo' haid.

THERAPIST. *(Opening HARRIET's file.)* Harriet, I am going to have to recommend to Mr. Brodas that you be removed from your present position and put in the fields to work where there is closer supervision.

HARRIET. Put me in de prison – I'ze gone. All de chains in de worl' cain't keep me now. My freedom ain't in the han's of you or Massuh Edward or eben in mah own han's. *(The THERAPIST is busy writing. HARRIET crosses to the door, and looks back.)* Mebbe I come back. When I do, mebbe I take your daughter.

(She exits, leaving the THERAPIST standing. Blackout)

THE END

HARRIET TUBMAN VISITS A THERAPIST

Floorplan

Backstage

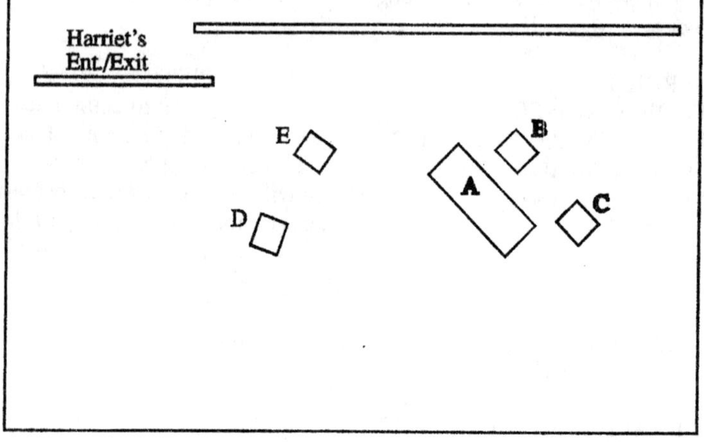

Audience

A, Therapist's Desk
B. Therapist's Chair
C. Filing Cabinet
D. Patient's Chair
E. Patient's Chair

MERIDIAN, MISSISSIPPI REDUX

by

Le Wilhelm

"THE PAST IS THE PAST, AND THE PRESENT IS NOW. THERE IS NO LOGIC IN BLAMING THOSE WHO COME AFTER FOR THE MISTAKES OF THEIR ANCESTORS, NOR IS THERE ANY LOGIC IN PRAISING THOSE WHO COME AFTER FOR THE HEROICS OF THEIR PREDECESSORS."

This play is dedicated to everyone who has met with prejudice because of the atrocities of the past.

MERIDIAN, MISSISSIPPI REDUX
by
Le Wilhelm

with

BRADLEY . . . . Kelly Morast

CORDELIA LeGRAND . . . . Sue Glausen-Smith

KIMBERLY WISE . . . . Kirsten Walsh

RAYMOND . . . . Ron Scott

Directed by Sharon Fallon

Produced by
Love Creek Productions, New York City

Special thanks to Sharon Fallon for having worked so hard with the timing and rhythm of this script and for all the other one-acts of mine to which she has given life over the years.

ABOUT THE AUTHOR

Other plays published by Samuel French, Inc. are *Strawberry Preserves, The Power and the Glory, Cherry Blend with Vanilla, Life Comes to the Old Maid, Whoppers, Tremulous* and *The Road to Ninevah. The Missouri Trilogy* is also represented by Samuel French, Inc. In addition to being a prolific playwright, Le Wilhelm also helps run Love Creek Production, directs, acts, serves as a judge for various playwriting competitions and enjoys participating in various arts festivals throughout the country.

CHARACTERS

> MRS. CORDELIA LeGRAND: White, 40's
> MISS KIMBERLY WISE: White, early 20's
> RAYMOND: Black, early 20's
> BRADLEY: White, early 20's

SETTING

> An old-world lovely Southern café.

(A restaurant in Meridian, Mississippi. MRS. LeGRAND is every bit the Southern lady. BRADLEY, the waiter, is a spirited young man, although somewhat effeminate.)

BRADLEY. Would you care for some more hot water for your tea?

MRS. LeGRAND. That would be nice, Bradley, thank you. And another wedge of lemon, if I might.

BRADLEY. Yes, ma'am.

(A young woman, early 20's, enters. She stands for a moment and looks around. She is not sure if she wants to go or stay.)

MRS. LeGRAND. Could I help you?

KIM. No.

MRS. LeGRAND. It's between breakfast and lunch, and I'm afraid the only waiter on the floor is bringing hot water for my tea.

KIM. I'm just looking around.

MRS. LeGRAND. I see.

KIM. Actually, you might be able to help me. Do you happen to know if this restaurant's been here for a while?

MRS. LeGRAND. Yes. Like everything and almost everyone here in Meridian, it's been here for a time. The Glass House has been here as long as I can remember.

KIM. That's its name?

MRS. LeGRAND. Yes. At one time, Momma says it was quite the talk of the southern part of the state. Before they invented plexiglass, it was rare to see so much glass in one building. I remember when one of the hurricanes blew through and practically demolished everything. Now it's all plexiglass. The last strong wind didn't do any damage at all. I think it might go back as far as the 1800's.

KIM. Back to when slaves had to wash all the windows.

MRS. LeGRAND. I don't know if it's quite that old. There aren't too many places here that go back that far.

KIM. But it's been here since the 50's?

MRS. LeGRAND. Of that I'm positive. You're not from Meridian, are you?

KIM. No.

MRS. LeGRAND. You have relatives here?

KIM. Just visiting.

MRS. LeGRAND. Passing through on your way to New Orleans?

KIM. No. Meridian., Mississippi is my sole destination.

MRS. LeGRAND. You're alone?

KIM. Yes.

MRS. LeGRAND. If you don't have other plans at the moment, you're more than welcome to join me. I'm having tea.

KIM. Oh, ah ... well, why not. I'm from New York City, and generally up there, you wouldn't just sit down with a total stranger, but I'm not up there now, so thank you.

MRS. LeGRAND. My name's Cordelia LeGrand.

KIM. Really?

MRS. LeGRAND. *(Responding to KIM's "nameshock.")* I know it's more than a little ostentatious.

KIM. I'm sorry ... it's just so ... so southern.

MRS. LeGRAND. *(Smiling)* I suppose it is.

KIM. It is, trust me!

MRS. LeGRAND. When I was a girl, I thoroughly despised my mother for giving it to me. Of course, my husband gave me the last name.

KIM. There's nothing wrong with it.

MRS. LeGRAND. Not now. I suppose. No, I suppose now it doesn't seem so inappropriate. But when you're a young girl. It was grandmother's and her grandmother's before her ... Lord only knows how far it goes back, probably all the way to King Lear. Mr. William Shakespeare's King Lear. And you are – ?

KIM. Kimberly. Kim Wise.

BRADLEY. Here's the hot water and the lemon. Oh, you have a guest?

MRS. LeGRAND. Yes, Bradley. This is Miss. It is Miss?

KIM. Yes.

MRS. LeGRAND. Miss Kimberly Wise.

BRADLEY. Pleased to meet you.

KIM. I'd like some coffee.

BRADLEY. Would you care to look at a menu?

KIM. No, Coffee's fine.

MRS. LeGRAND. They have wonderful desserts here. In fact, The Glass House is known for its desserts. Some of the recipes go back years and years.

KIM. Okay, let me see a menu.

BRADLEY. Yes, ma'am.

(He exits.)

KIM. Does he call everyone "ma'am"?

MRS. LeGRAND. We do that down here. So you're visiting all the way from New York City?

KIM. That's right.

MRS. LeGRAND. I've never visited there.

KIM. I would imagine it's not a very popular place around here.

MRS. LeGRAND. Why do you say that?

KIM. Southerners aren't all that fond of Northerners.

MRS. LeGRAND. It's difficult for some people, I suppose. They don't understand how people from other places relate differently.

KIM. I suppose you're wondering why I came here?

MRS. LeGRAND. Most young people go to New Orleans or to the Florida Gulf.

KIM. This is where my parents met.

MRS. LeGRAND. Here in Meridian?

KIM. Yes.

MRS. LeGRAND. Are they southern?

KIM. Hardly. They were down here in the 50's when they were young.

MRS. LeGRAND. Oh.

KIM. Uh huh.

MRS. LeGRAND. Were they helping with voter registration?

KIM. As a matter of fact.

MRS. LeGRAND. There were actually quite a few people who came.

KIM. Do you want me to sit someplace else?

MRS. LeGRAND. Why would I want you to move to another table?

KIM. My parents weren't exactly welcomed with open arms.

MRS. LeGRAND. Oh, I see.

KIM. They don't talk a great deal about it, but I suspect they're lucky to have gotten out alive.

MRS. LeGRAND. It was a very difficult time.

KIM. Especially for the African-Americans.

MRS. LeGRAND. That's true ... but for everyone ... your parents, I would think.

KIM. I'm very proud of them.

MRS. LeGRAND. It was a very chaotic time. The rules were all changing.

KIM. For the better.

MRS. LeGRAND. I was young then. A little younger than your parents, I would imagine. It was very frightening.

BRADLEY. Your coffee, ma'am. And a dessert menu.

KIM. Is that cream?

BRADLEY. *(Smiling)* Yes, ma'am. We always serve real cream here at the Glass House.

KIM. Could I have skim milk. If you don't mind.

BRADLEY. I'll get it for you.

MRS. LeGRAND. Thank you, Bradley.

KIM. I didn't think anyone served cream anymore.

MRS. LeGRAND. It's a specialty of the Glass House.

KIM. Down here I suppose old ways die slow.

MRS. LeGRAND. Some of them do. And hopefully some of them never will.

KIM. Mom and Dad said it'd be like stepping back in time.

MRS. LeGRAND. You must be very proud of them.

KIM. Yes, I am! What they did was important. I like to think they helped bring about a change, helping give human beings their basic rights.

MRS. LeGRAND. It must be wonderful to have parents you can look up to like that.

KIM. Yes. I've read every newspaper and magazine that I can get my hands on from when they were down here. Yesterday, I went to the Meridian Public Library.

MRS. LeGRAND. If you get a chance, there's a whole section devoted to Meridian at the University Library. It's very thorough.

KIM. You've been?

MRS. LeGRAND. Yes, a couple of years ago.

KIM. But weren't you here then?

MRS. LeGRAND. I was young. At the end, I didn't know what was happening. I just remember that it was like a war. It was as if the Civil War was happening all over again.

KIM. At least the right side keeps winning.

BRADLEY. Have you selected a dessert, ma'am?

KIM. I'm afraid I haven't even looked.

BRADLEY. I'll check back later.

KIM. He's nice looking.

MRS. LeGRAND. Bradley?

KIM. Who else?

MRS. LeGRAND. I think so.

KIM. It's a shame he's gay.

MRS. LeGRAND. What?

KIM. Homosexual.

MRS. LeGRAND. Oh.

KIM. I mean it's a shame for women that he is. Not that there's anything wrong with being gay. But, well, I'm young, he's my age, he's nice looking. You know what I mean.

MRS. LeGRAND. Yes. How do you know he's homosexual?

KIM. I can tell.

MRS. LeGRAND. How?

KIM. You know. The walk. The way he holds his head, the way he looks at me. It's different.

MRS. LeGRAND. I see.

KIM. There are a lot of gays in New York, so a girl gets used to being able to spot them.

MRS. LeGRAND. Spot them?

KIM. So she's not wasting her time.

MRS. LeGRAND. You wouldn't want to waste your time on – ?

KIM. I don't mean it like that. I have gay friends. Everyone who lives in New York has gay friends. You know he's not going to be ... you know what I mean. Believe it or not, a town of this size, I'll guarantee you there are a number of homosexuals here.

MRS. LeGRAND. Yes, I know. I'm not that out of touch with reality. I'm just not sure that Bradley is gay.

KIM. Trust me, he is! I can tell. I suppose I shouldn't be talking about something like this. I don't want to shock you.

MRS. LeGRAND. You're not shocking me. I suppose there's always been men with a more gentle nature.

KIM. *(Laughs)* Gentle nature? You wouldn't think "gentle nature" if you saw some of them in the city.

MRS. LeGRAND. Perhaps. But we're in Meridian, Mississippi right now. And despite what you might have heard about us, there are certain aspects of our culture that you probably don't understand.

KIM. Such as?

MRS. LeGRAND. We have the tendency to look at those among us who are different with a certain amount of pride. It's a southern thing. And I'm certainly not speaking for everyone. I guess I'm speaking more of the old families now. We see our gentlemen that way. I'm sure you've heard it said that we're not ashamed of our mentally ill. In fact, any of the old families that didn't have at least a touch of neuroticism here and there would hang its head in shame. Perhaps we feel this way about our sensitive men and our relatives who are "different," because they're proof positive that there is something gentle and worthwhile that exists in the blood of our family. No, we're terribly proud of our gentle, our lost souls whose very natures cannot stand the harsh glare of reality. I'm sure this doesn't make much sense. And I am not at all convinced that Bradley is gay. But that's neither here nor there. Perhaps we should talk about something else. The garden here is lovely, don't you think?

KIM. What?

MRS. LeGRAND. *(Gesturing)* The garden.

KIM. Yes, it's very pretty.

MRS. LeGRAND. I think so.

KIM. What are those bright flowers? I see them all over the place.

MRS. LeGRAND. *(Pointing)* Those?

KIM. Yes.

MRS. LeGRAND. Those are azaleas. The bright pink buds just about to bloom are crepe myrtles. I especially like crepes. Lovely name for a flower, I think. But I'm not sure why.

KIM. Carnations and roses are about the only flowers I can identify.

MRS. LeGRAND. I hope you don't have allergies. All the blossoms can play havoc with them.

KIM. No. I like the Spanish moss.

MRS. LeGRAND. People from out of state always seem to love the moss.

KIM. Don't you?

MRS. LeGRAND. I've lived here all my life. It's always been around me. It just seems so ... the way it is ... normal.

KIM. I'm going to take some back.

MRS. LeGRAND. If you do, be careful. There's a lot of insects that live in it. I'm sure you wouldn't want them in your home. You know, if you really want to see beautiful flowers and Spanish moss so think you can't see the trees, you should go to the old cemetery.

KIM. Is it close by?

MRS. LeGRAND. Just a couple of blocks. Turn right on Bayou Avenue, you can't miss it. It'll be ablaze with blossoms, and the live oak trees are among the oldest in town. I'm sure they go back way before the Civil War. And the statuary is ... well ... very southern. Down here we've always had a thing about making sure our dead aren't forgotten. The place is a-mob with angels and gargoyles and statues of the long forgotten.

(A nice looking black man, around 20, enters.)

MRS. LeGRAND. Raymond, I'm glad you're here.

RAYMOND. What is it?

MRS. LeGRAND. Raymond, this is Miss Kimberly Wise.

KIM. Kim.

RAYMOND. Pleased to meet you, ma'am.

KIM. You certainly do say "ma'am" a lot down here.

MRS. LeGRAND. Kim's from New York City. She was kind enough to join me for my mid-morning tea so I didn't have to sit alone.

RAYMOND. New York City?

KIM. Yes.

RAYMOND. What brought you down here to Meridian?

KIM. My parents first met here. A long time ago.

RAYMOND. Are they here with you?

KIM. No. I came alone.

MRS. LeGRAND. Raymond, I need for you to pick up some things from the Garden Center next door. Some rose powder, some Miracle Gro, Everything's on this list.

RAYMOND. Okay.

MRS. LeGRAND. And here are the keys to the trunk, if you'll put everything back there.

RAYMOND. On my way.

MRS. LeGRAND. Don't forget to bring back the keys.

RAYMOND. Right.

MRS. LeGRAND. Don't forget.

RAYMOND. *(Pleasantly)* I heard you.

MRS. LeGRAND. And hurry. Don't go over there and start talking. I need to dust the roses as soon as possible. If I don't get it taken care of this afternoon, I'm going to lose most of the new blossoms.

RAYMOND. I'll be right back.

(He exits. KIM is upset.)

KIM. He seems like a nice man.

MRS. LeGRAND. He is.

KIM. Is that what you really think?

MRS. LeGRAND. Why, yes.

KIM. That's certainly not how you were acting.

MRS. LeGRAND. What are you trying to say?

KIM. I think you know.

MRS. LeGRAND. No I don't.

KIM. The way you spoke to him.

MRS. LeGRAND. I really don't know what you mean.

KIM. You were ordering him around like you were some plantation owner before the Civil War.

MRS. LeGRAND. What?

KIM. You don't even realize it, do you?

MRS. LeGRAND. There's nothing to realize.

KIM. My parents said it'd be this way. That I had to realize that you people aren't knowingly evil. That you're so set in your ways that you don't even realize what you're doing.

MRS. LeGRAND. I can't tell you how wrong you are.

KIM. No, I'm not. Didn't you hear yourself? All that stuff about bringing back your precious keys. What did you think, that he was going to steal your car and sell it to some thugs? Or maybe he'd just take it and go joy riding? OR maybe he'd use it to get the hell out of here? I certainly couldn't blame him for that. I don't see how the African-Americans can stand it down here with you people and how you behave.

MRS. LeGRAND. You don't know how wrong you are.

KIM. I know how right I am! When my mother and father came down here, they had to fight for people to have the basic rights which are guaranteed by the Constitution. Rights like being able to sit in restaurants, to vote, to sit where they chose on buses. But how much have things really changed? Oh, you might not use the "N" word, except behind closed doors, but it's there in your mind, cloistered in all your southern charms. And you know, you almost had me fooled. I thought you were a decent person until I saw you in action. But now I feel like I should go and have a bath just from having shared a table with you!

(RAYMOND enters.)

RAYMOND. Jessie said you'd have to tell him what the problems with the roses were before he'd know what powder you needed.

KIM. *(In preparation to leave.)* I'm sorry, would you please excuse me. I can't stand anymore of this.

RAYMOND. What's wrong?

KIM. *(Placing money on table.)* This should cover my coffee.

RAYMOND. Has something happened I don't know about?

KIM. What has happened is that I've seen with my own eyes the way the whites treat you, and I'm disgusted.

RAYMOND. What's she talking about, Mother?

MRS. LeGRAND. I'm afraid there's been a misunderstanding.

KIM. Mother!?!?

MRS. LeGRAND. That's what I've been –

KIM. Why did you call her "Mother?"

RAYMOND. Because she is my mother. I was adopted when I was only a few weeks old.

KIM. Is that true?

MRS. LeGRAND. Raymond is my son. And the reason I said that about the keys is because the last time I gave him my keys he forgot to return them, and I had to call a cab to take me all the way home and then bring me back to the car with the spare set.

KIM. I feel like a fool.

MRS. LeGRAND. You should.

RAYMOND. Did you think Mother was some kind of bigot?

MRS. LeGRAND. Aphids. Tell Jessie I have aphids, Son.

RAYMOND. Aphids.

MRS. LeGRAND. Go on and pick up the –

RAYMOND. Are you going to be alright here?

MRS. LeGRAND. I'm fine, Son. Go on.

(He exits.)

KIM. I owe you an apology.

MRS. LeGRAND. Yes, you do. And because of who your parents were, I'll accept it.

KIM. Thank you.

MRS. LeGRAND. But Miss Wise, you really do need to be careful. It's very easy, in an attempt to fight bigotry, to become a bigot yourself. Perhaps you should learn that bigotry's not an inherited quality. You have to treat each person as an individual.

KIM. I know. You're right.

MRS. LeGRAND. Yes, I am. Sometimes that's very hard to do. Just like it's hard for someone who's been raised a racist to really understand how wrong racism is. It's very difficult for some people not to blame and condemn whole groups for the sins of their ancestors. It's not hereditary.

KIM. I guess.

MRS. LeGRAND. It's not. From what you say, your parents were heroes. I would like to meet them. You have every reason to be very proud of them. But you don't inherit their heroism. That's their contribution. You have to make your own. I really should go over to the Garden Center and make sure Jessie has the rose powder I need.

(When she stands, we notice for the first time that she walks with a cane. It should be a nice cane. BRADLEY comes over.)

BRADLEY. Are you going?

MRS. LeGRAND. Yes. I want to make sure Jessie has the right powder for my roses. Besides, I want to get out of here before the lunchtime arrival of the duennas of southern tradition.

BRADLEY. You're lucky.

MRS. LeGRAND. Very.

BRADLEY. Did you decide if you wanted dessert?

KIM. I don't –

MRS. LeGRAND. Bradley, bring her the Glass House Special. *(To KIM.)* It's a very old, very southern recipe. You don't have to eat it all, but you should taste it. Put it on my tab, Bradley.

KIM. I couldn't –

MRS. LeGRAND. I insist. You know, I could have met your parents. I'm not sure. I don't remember a great deal from that time. And don't forget to visit the old cemetery. I can assure you, you'll never have seen anything quite like it. It's been most interesting. Take care.

KIM. Goodbye.

BRADLEY. Is she upset about something?

KIM. I'm afraid I made a horrible mistake. I feel dreadful.

BRADLEY. Oh?

KIM. My parents were here in the late 50's to help with voter registration, and we were talking about that time.

BRADLEY. It was a very upsetting time for her.

KIM. I misunderstood how ... I didn't know Raymond was her son. I thought she was being racist with him.

BRADLEY. Oh, my. It's a wonder she didn't whack you with her cane.

KIM. I feel terrible.

BRADLEY. Did she tell you anything about back then?

KIM. No.

BRADLEY. About what happened to her?

KIM. To her?

BRADLEY. If she didn't tell you, maybe I shouldn't either, but you'll probably never see her again. If you do, don't say anything.

KIM. Alright.

BRADLEY. Now this was before I was born, but I've heard all the stories. I think she was around 14 years old, and there was a sit-in scheduled for a lunch counter over in Philadelphia.

KIM. Philadelphia?

BRADLEY. Philadelphia, Mississippi. There were a couple of older kids that were planning to go and join the Negroes, and they were supposed to come by and get her. Of course, her family knew nothing about this. And when the others didn't show up, she snuck out of the house and jumped in her mother's car and drove it all the way over to Philadelphia.

KIM. At 14?

BRADLEY. That's the story. Now when she got there, the others weren't there. She ended up being the only white person. Now most 14-year-olds would have gotten scared and run, but she joined right in. And when the police came, there were problems and she ended up being beaten so badly that she was in a coma for almost two weeks. That's why she has the cane.

KIM. Oh my God.

BRADLEY. After she came out of the coma, it took her over a year to recover. The physical injury was bad enough, but the mental trauma ... she spent almost a year in a private asylum in Hattiesburg. She doesn't remember much about the day of the sit-in.

KIM. I see.

BRADLEY. But two years later, although she walked with a cane, she was present at the cotillion in Jackson and met my father. The scandal of the adoption came later.

KIM. Met your father?

BRADLEY. Yes. She's my mom. I thought you knew.

KIM. No.

BRADLEY. I wonder why she didn't tell you. I just assumed you knew. She's about as stubborn as they get, but she's a wonderful person.

KIM. I'm afraid I've done something else rather stupid.

BRADLEY. What?

KIM. I had no idea you were her son.

BRADLEY. So?

KIM. I'm afraid I told her you were gay.

BRADLEY. You told her what?

KIM. I told her you were gay. Please tell me that she already knew. That you've already told her. I had no idea she was your mother.

BRADLEY. *(Laughing)* You told her I was gay?

KIM. Yes.

BRADLEY. *(Laughing harder.)* What did she say?

KIM. What is so funny?

BRADLEY. Just tell me what she said.

KIM. She questioned whether I was right.

BRADLEY. I bet she did!

KIM. I don't understand.

BRADLEY. I'm sure she wouldn't care if I were. But I'm not gay.

KIM. *(Not really knowing what she's saying.)* Yes, you are.

BRADLEY. No, I'm not. And without going into personal history, let's just say Mother has had to deal with some problems that make her all too aware of the fact that I like women.

KIM. Well, I was sure –

BRADLEY. Sorry.

KIM. No, I'm the one that's sorry.

BRADLEY. No harm done. Don't worry about it. I've got to run and get your Glass House Special. Mother will ask if you liked it. And then I've got to get ready for lunch and the old guard. *(He exits and returns quickly with the dessert.)* Here you go. I'll warn you, it's terribly rich. Would you like more coffee?

KIM. No, I'm fine. *(She tastes.)* This is delicious.

BRADLEY. If you don't have anywhere to go, you should stay for awhile. They'll be arriving shortly. The true remnants of the old south. You've got to see it to believe it. *(As he is exiting.)* Enjoy your dessert.

THE END

PROPERTY PLOT

2 fancy teacups and saucers
Fancy creamer and sugar bowl
Cloth napkins
Fancy dessert plate
Slice of Mississippi Mud Cake
Car Keys
Lemons
Shopping List
Cane

COSTUME PLOT

CORDELIA:
Pastel flowered dress with short sleeves; hat; gloves; small beige handbag; light colored mid-heel shoes.

BRADLEY:
Black trousers; white tux shirt; black bow tie; white waiter's jacket.

RAYMOND:
Light khaki short sleeved shirt; dark khaki trousers; brown shoes.

KIM:
Jeans; white T-shirt; oversized demin shirt; large backpack/handbag.

STUDIO PORTRAIT

by

Arlene Hutton

for Don

STUDIO PORTRAIT was first produced by The Journey Company at the American Living Room Series at HERE in July, 1996, directed by Mark Roberts, stage managed by Nancy Bell with:

ABIGAIL . . . . Beth Lincks

ROBERT . . . . Michael James Reed

STUDIO PORTRAIT was presented by The Journey Company at the Edinburgh Festival Fringe in August, 1996 and at the Footlights Players for the Piccolo Spoleto Festival in Charleston, South Carolina, May 24 – June 7, 1997, directed by Mark Roberts with original music by Daniel J. Adkins, Costumes were by Shelley Norton. Wade Howard was production stage manager at Piccolo Spoleto. The cast was as follows:

ABIGAIL . . . . Beth Lincks

ROBERT . . . . Michael James Reed

STUDIO PORTRAIT was restaged by the Journey Company at the Henry Street Settlement Experimental Space for the first New York International Fringe Festival, a production of The Present Company, August 13-24, 1997, directed by Margot Avery. Lights were by Christopher Gorzelnik, original music was by Daniel J. Adkins and costumes were by Shelley Norton. Jim Pelegano was production stage manager and Marc Hoppe and Stephen Alderfer were assistants. This restaging was then presented at the Harold Clurman Theatre, New York City. The cast was as follows:

ABIGAIL . . . . Beth Lincks

ROBERT . . . . Arthur Hanket

Special thanks to Judith Royer, Allison Korman, Carla Cantrelle and all the members of The Journey Company. Extra special thanks to Scott McLucas, Elizabeth Falk, Veronica Kehoe, Stephen Fife and Kristine Niven. Thanks also to the staffs of the American Living Room, Edinburgh Festival Fringe, Piccolo Spoleto, the Peekaboo Festival, New York International Fringe Festival and the Samuel French Short Plays Festival. And to Artistic New Directions, The Players, Traveling Light Productions and New Dramatists. Thanks, as always, to Susann Brinkley, Yolanda Smith and the Alice's Fourth Floor playwriting groups.

ABOUT THE AUTHOR

Arlene Hutton became a member of New Dramatists in 1998. She began writing plays five years earlier at Alice's Fourth Floor under the direction of Susann Brinkley. Hutton's short plays, including the award-winning *I Dream Before I Take The Stand*, have been performed at university and regional theatres around the country. Evenings of her collected one-acts have been presented by Beth Lincks and The Journey Company at the Edinburgh Festival Fringe, Piccolo Spoleto, the New York International Fringe Festival and the Philadelphia Fringe Festival, directed by Judith Royer, Mark Roberts, Beth Lincks, Vivian Sorenson, Michael Gellman and Margot Avery. New York credits include Circle-in-the-Square Downtown, Alice's Fourth Floor, Cherry Lane Theatre, Red Earth Ensemble, Neighborhood Playhouse, HERE, 78th Street Theatre Lab and West Bank Downstairs Theatre. Hutton is a member of The LAB Theatre Company and was a participating artist at Alice's Fourth Floor. *Last Train To Nibroc,* her first full-length work, was workshopped at the New York International Fringe Festival in 1998 at the Henry Street Settlement Recital Hall, directed by Michael Montel and produced by The Journey Company. Arlene Hutton is represented by literary agent Donald Maass.

CHARACTERS

ABIGAIL:
> 30's or 40's. Almost pretty, only slightly neurotic and a little nervous.

ROBERT:
> A photographer about the same age. A really nice guy.

PLACE

An Upper West Side studio apartment.

TIME

The present.

(Like a camera flash going off, lights come up suddenly on a make-shift photographer's set up in a studio apartment. A sofa to one side. An umbrella light or two. Possibly a backdrop. ROBERT is behind a camera on a tripod, with equipment beside him on a rolling table. ABIGAIL is sitting on a stool, being photographed. There is a click as ROBERT snaps a picture.)

ABIGAIL. I blinked. Sorry. I blinked.

ROBERT. *(Putting down the camera.)* That's okay. We'll take a break.

ABIGAIL. *(Overlapping)* I keep blinking. I'm sorry.

ROBERT. It's natural. Stop for now.

ABIGAIL. I can keep going.

ROBERT. No need. Take a break.

ABIGAIL. I don't want to take up your –

ROBERT. *(Smiling)* Maybe I need a break, too.

ABIGAIL. I didn't think about –

ROBERT. That's okay.

ABIGAIL. You can get really self-absorbed. Being photographed.

ROBERT. I guess so.

ABIGAIL. I see why models seem so selfish.

ROBERT. Maybe. *(He starts towards the kitchen offstage.)* Something to drink?

ABIGAIL. *(Relaxing her pose.)* I'm just not used to this.

ROBERT. No one is.

ABIGAIL. Well, models.

ROBERT. Well, yes.

ABIGAIL. They're used to ...

ROBERT. Yeah. *(Walking offstage to the kitchen.)* Coke? Perrier? Evian?

ABIGAIL. Anything. Don't you find?

ROBERT. Which?

ABIGAIL. Don't you find that models?

ROBERT. *(Walking back on with a couple of bottles of mineral water, different brands.)* Which do you want to drink? I don't often work with professional models.

ABIGAIL. But you're ...?

ROBERT. Corporate stuff.

ABIGAIL. Which is?

ROBERT. Usually buildings. What do you want to drink? Buildings and rooms.

ABIGAIL. Oh, not people? Oh, Perrier.

ROBERT. Sometimes a ...
ABIGAIL. *(Prompting)* Products?
ROBERT. Not for ads. Just for in-house stuff. Annual reports.
ABIGAIL. No people?
ROBERT. Oh, the CEO in his office. Like that. High-priced real estate. Not studio portraits.
ABIGAIL. But you're doing ...
ROBERT. I was surprised to get a call for portrait work. But it's a slow week. Holiday weekend.
ABIGAIL. Yeah, right.

(Pause)

ROBERT. So, how did you happen to – You said –
ABIGAIL. I had your card.
ROBERT. Oh, yeah. Right.
ABIGAIL. I called because I had your card.
ROBERT. Yeah.
ABIGAIL. You're very good. I mean, good to work with.
ROBERT. Thanks. *(He sits down with his drink.)* Yeah, it's fun to do studio work occasionally. But not for a steady diet.
ABIGAIL. No? You'd rather ... what?
ROBERT. Be outside.
ABIGAIL. I see.
ROBERT. You spend lots of time in the darkroom.
ABIGAIL. Of course.
ROBERT. And if you're in a studio as well ...
ABIGAIL. *(Overlapping)* Of course, you wouldn't ...
ROBERT. *(Continuing)* You'd never get outside.
ABIGAIL. I see.
ROBERT. So I like to travel around.
ABIGAIL. Abroad?
ROBERT. *(Smiling)* No, just around. New York, Jersey, sometimes Connecticut.
ABIGAIL. *(Smiling)* That's good.
ROBERT. *(Smiling at her.)* Yeah, I like it.
ABIGAIL. You do well, then.
ROBERT. I've been lucky.
ABIGAIL. Good. That's good. Lots of corporate stuff. And buildings.
ROBERT. Yes.
ABIGAIL. You don't miss doing people.
ROBERT. Well, like I said, I do it occasionally.
ABIGAIL. Like now.
ROBERT. Yes.
ABIGAIL. And it's fun?

ROBERT. Today?
ABIGAIL. No, I mean people, well, yes.
ROBERT. Today's a nice shoot, yeah.
ABIGAIL. No, I didn't mean –
ROBERT. No, it's okay.
ABIGAIL. I'm not good at having my –
ROBERT. You're fine. Don't get self-conscious on me now. We still have two rolls to go.

(He puts down his drink and begins resetting his equipment.)

ABIGAIL. Yeah. Right. *(Pause)* You're very good at putting people at ease.
ROBERT. It's part of the challenge.
ABIGAIL. Oh. Is that why you like buildings?
ROBERT. *(Laughing)* Oh, they have their own challenges.
ABIGAIL. *(Laughing)* Do people walk in front of the buildings while you're shooting?
ROBERT. Well, yes, but that doesn't matter.
ABIGAIL. But doesn't that spoil ...
ROBERT. The shot? No. Not with a slow speed.
ABIGAIL. I don't understand.
ROBERT. With a slow shutter speed the people don't appear in the picture.
ABIGAIL. You erase them?
ROBERT. No. I'll explain, well, see, you put the camera on a tripod. No, well, first, um, if you move your arm quickly while I'm taking your picture we'll get a blur, right?
ABIGAIL. Okay.
ROBERT. If I photograph a race horse I have to use a very fast shutter speed.
ABIGAIL. Okay.
ROBERT. When I photograph a building I use a very slow shutter speed.
ABIGAIL. Doesn't that blur the people?
ROBERT. No, well, yes. But if the speed is so long, say several minutes, the people blur so much ...
ABIGAIL. They disappear
ROBERT. That's right.
ABIGAIL. But they walked in front of the camera.
ROBERT. But the camera sees the building for so long and the people for so short a time.
ABIGAIL. Uh huh.
ROBERT. The building sort of wins out.
ABIGAIL. Wow. The people don't exist.

ROBERT. Not to the camera.
ABIGAIL. Wow. *(She smiles.)* Learn something new every day.
ROBERT. Ready to start again?

(He takes her drink from her.)

ABIGAIL. Oh. Sure. Wait. My hair ...
ROBERT. It's fine. Just touch up your lipstick.
ABIGAIL. Right. *(Reaching for her bag.)* I don't have this color.
ROBERT. *(Fixing the camera.)* What?
ABIGAIL. My make-up. I had it done on my way here. *(As she gets out a compact and lipstick and looks at herself.)* My hair, too. This morning. I don't usually look like this. I had my make-up done. So I don't have this color lipstick anymore. They tried to sell me some –
ROBERT. I'm shooting black and white.

(He picks up the Polaroid camera.)

ABIGAIL. Oh, of course. How silly of me. They tried to sell –
ROBERT. That's okay. You look fine.

(They laugh together. He snaps a picture with the Polaroid.)

ABIGAIL. Oh! I didn't know you were starting.
ROBERT. You look beautiful.
ABIGAIL. No.
ROBERT. Yes, you do.
ABIGAIL. But I'm not.
ROBERT. Look at this Polaroid.

(He picks up a developed picture off the table and hands it to her.)

ABIGAIL. Good lighting.
ROBERT. Come on.
ABIGAIL. No, actually you're right. It looks pretty good.
ROBERT. See?
ABIGAIL. *(Looking at the picture.)* This is okay.
ROBERT. Good. *(He takes the picture from her.)* You're much more relaxed. *(He gets behind the camera.)* That's good. Drop your, yeah, like that. Good.

(A click. He keeps shooting when appropriate throughout the following.)

ABIGAIL. I was nervous at first.
ROBERT. Everyone is.

ABIGAIL. But you're very good.
ROBERT. This is good. Tilt the ... yes. Oh, wait.
ABIGAIL. What?
ROBERT. *(He steps to her and gently brushes something away from her brow.)* A hair. There. *(He touches her shoulders.)* And down. Breathe.
ABIGAIL. *(Exhales)* Right. Okay.
ROBERT. Think about your favorite baby animal.
ABIGAIL. My what?
ROBERT. Baby animals.
ABIGAIL. Kittens?
ROBERT. Good. And chin ... good. And ... good. And good ...
ABIGAIL. Kittens! This is fun now.
ROBERT. Twist a little. Other way. Good. And good. And ... wait. The hair.
ABIGAIL. What?

(She starts to brush it away, but he gets to her in time and does it himself.)

ROBERT. Got it.
ABIGAIL. This is work.
ROBERT. Good. *(He returns to the camera and begins to shoot again.)* Think about the kittens.
ABIGAIL. Kittens!
ROBERT. Good. *(They laugh and he shoots some pictures.)* Very good.
ABIGAIL. This is fun. I feel like a model. This roll's going to be the good one.
ROBERT. There's always a few good shots right in the beginning.
ABIGAIL. *(Still posing.)* Uh-huh.
ROBERT. And then a whole roll that's just worthless.
ABIGAIL. Uh-huh.
ROBERT. Then the best ones at the end. *(He looks up from the camera.)* Stop for a minute.
ABIGAIL. What?
ROBERT. Breathe.
ABIGAIL. Oh, right.
ROBERT. *(Laughing)* Yeah, right.
ABIGAIL. Breathe.
ROBERT. Look around the room.
ABIGAIL. What?
ROBERT. *(As he's adjusting a lens.)* So you don't over-focus —
ABIGAIL. On the camera. I see.

(Looks around the room.)

ROBERT. *(Adjusting a light.)* Right.

ABIGAIL. Great place.
ROBERT. I've been real happy here.
ABIGAIL. You've been here a long time.
ROBERT. Ten years.

(He adjusts his tripod.)

ABIGAIL. Wow.
ROBERT. It's been good.
ABIGAIL. You ever want a bigger place?
ROBERT. No, not in the city. I've got a house upstate. I mostly live there.
ABIGAIL. How nice.
ROBERT. It's great.

(He focuses the camera.)

ABIGAIL. Where?
ROBERT. Greene County.
ABIGAIL. Oh, how nice.
ROBERT. Oh, it's great.
ABIGAIL. Pretty there.
ROBERT. It's great. *(He starts to shoot her again.)* Like that, good. *(A couple more shutter clicks.)* That's it.

(He stops shooting.)

ABIGAIL. That's all?
ROBERT. Change film.

(He goes to the table and changes the film through the following.)

ABIGAIL. Oh, good.
ROBERT. You're having a good time.
ABIGAIL. Yeah, now.
ROBERT. You can slump for a minute.
ABIGAIL. *(Still in a stiff pose.)* I can ... ? *(She laughs.)* You're right. This gets easier.
ROBERT. Good. *(Pause)* Why don't you change?
ABIGAIL. Change what?
ROBERT. Jackets. You brought another –
ABIGAIL. Oh, that's right. *(She looks around.)* Where's my – Here. *(Picking up her bag.)* I brought a couple.
ROBERT. Whichever.
ABIGAIL. I don't know which color.

(She takes off her cardigan.)

    ROBERT. It's black and white.
    ABIGAIL. Of course.
    ROBERT. You didn't ask for color.
    ABIGAIL. No. They said black and white.

(She pulls a jacket out of her bag.)

    ROBERT. The publication.
    ABIGAIL. The magazine.
    ROBERT. Did you need color for anything else? I can shoot a color roll.
    ABIGAIL. I don't think so.
    ROBERT. For relatives, Christmas cards?
    ABIGAIL. No, that's okay.
    ROBERT. I'm not pushing.
    ABIGAIL. Oh, I didn't mean –
    ROBERT. I'd rather stick with black and white.
    ABIGAIL. Why? Is my –
    ROBERT. Don't have to change the lights.
    ABIGAIL. They're different?
    ROBERT. A little.
    ABIGAIL. I guess if I'd thought about that, I'd realized ...
    ROBERT. So, which jacket?
    ABIGAIL. The dressy one?

(She holds it up.)

    ROBERT. That's good. A different look.
    ABIGAIL. Earrings?
    ROBERT. Let's see.
    ABIGAIL. *(Holding them up.)* These?
    ROBERT. Yeah, that's good.
    ABIGAIL. So, this jacket.
    ROBERT. Let's see it on.
    ABIGAIL. *(As she puts the jacket on.)* I'm glad I brought –
    ROBERT. It's always a good idea to have choices.
    ABIGAIL. I didn't think about it. Until you said on the phone.
    ROBERT. Choices are good.
    ABIGAIL. What about a scarf?

(She starts to pull it out of her bag but doesn't put it on.)

    ROBERT. *(Busy with the film.)* No. Too much around the neck. Scarves look great in real life when we see them move, but it's too static for film. Just looks bulky. Like some hair styles. You need to see the movement for it to work.

ABIGAIL. Wow. I guess that's why you like buildings. Taking pictures of buildings. They don't move.

(She sits back on the stool.)

ROBERT. *(Laughing)* Never thought about it. Maybe you're right. Buildings are sure easier than, say, children or small animals.

ABIGAIL. Kittens!

ROBERT. I've created a monster. Good jacket. Let's get going while you're relaxed.

ABIGAIL. Kittens.

ROBERT. Good ... chin ... good jacket ... other side ... good.

(He starts shooting again. He may have the camera off the tripod at this point and be moving around more.)

ABIGAIL. I love it up there.

(She looks more relaxed than ever before.)

ROBERT. Where?

ABIGAIL. Greene County.

ROBERT. Me, too. Turn more to me.

ABIGAIL. Where?

ROBERT. Left shoulder.

ABIGAIL. No, where's your –

ROBERT. Actually not far from Woodstock.

ABIGAIL. *(Laughing)* No.

ROBERT. Shoulder and, good, oh, good.

ABIGAIL. Woodstock.

ROBERT. Good, just move however ... good.

ABIGAIL. My favorite restaurant –

ROBERT. The Bear?

(Still clicking.)

ABIGAIL. Yes!

ROBERT. It's great.

ABIGAIL. You have a house.

ROBERT. And some acreage.

ABIGAIL. That's great.

ROBERT. I converted a garage. Into the lens. Good.

ABIGAIL. Into a studio? The garage?

ROBERT. Right.
ABIGAIL. That's great.
ROBERT. Chin down a little now. Great.
ABIGAIL. Animals?
ROBERT. A dog and two cats.
ABIGAIL. Kittens?
ROBERT. I hope not!

(Still shooting.)

ABIGAIL. Kittens!
ROBERT. *(Laughing)* Good. That's very good. Right to me. Great! *(Click)* Okay.
ABIGAIL. That's it?
ROBERT. That's the roll. That's it.

(He removes the film.)

ABIGAIL. Oh.

(She stays seated on the stool.)

ROBERT. You want another? I think you've got quite a few good shots to choose from.
ABIGAIL. Well, I only need one picture.
ROBERT. For the ...
ABIGAIL. Magazine. It's a story. About me. Trade magazine.
ROBERT. *(Taking the camera off the tripod, etc.)* You said when you called.
ABIGAIL. It's not a big deal. But they wanted a picture. I didn't have one. I needed a picture.
ROBERT. When, exactly?
ABIGAIL. For next month. There's no hurry.
ROBERT. *(Still dealing with equipment.)* The proofs will be ready on Friday.
ABIGAIL. And your idea about relatives. Send some pictures for Christmas.
ROBERT. You'll have plenty of time to get them.
ABIGAIL. The proofs.
ROBERT. I can mail them to you.
ABIGAIL. I can pick them up.
ROBERT. Oh, okay. *(Getting a card off a desk.)* Here's the photo lab address.

(He hands her the card.)

ABIGAIL. I can pick them up here.
ROBERT. *(As he goes back to the table.)* I won't be in town.
ABIGAIL. I'll have to choose.
ROBERT. Well, the lab will send me a copy, too.

(He puts the film into a professional photo lab envelope.)

ABIGAIL. Good.
ROBERT. I'll go over it, go over the proofs, um, and I can fax you –
do you have a –
ABIGAIL. A fax? Yes.
ROBERT. Um, I'll fax you a copy of the proofs. I'll circle the numbers
I like. Just compare it with the proof sheet you get from the lab. So you've
got a fax.
ABIGAIL. Yes.
ROBERT. Do you have a loupe?
ABIGAIL. A what?
ROBERT. Magnifier?
ABIGAIL. I don't think so.
ROBERT. *(Picking one up.)* Like this?
ABIGAIL. Oh, one of – no.
ROBERT. You could look at the proofs at the lab.
ABIGAIL. When will you be back in the city?
ROBERT. Probably a month. I usually don't come in the summer. You
call me in the country if you have any questions.
ABIGAIL. Or I might be driving up there.
ROBERT. Really?
ABIGAIL. Some friends have a rental.
ROBERT. Well, then, you could stop by.
ABIGAIL. Okay.
ROBERT. See the dog.
ABIGAIL. And the cats.
ROBERT. Yeah, the cats. Call me. I'll let you know.
ABIGAIL. What's the number?
ROBERT. It's on the card.
ABIGAIL. No.
ROBERT. You have my card.
ABIGAIL. There's just this number. The number here.

(Getting a card out of her bag.)

ROBERT. No, there's both.
ABIGAIL. *(She holds up the card.)* No, just the city –
ROBERT. You have a –
ABIGAIL. What?

ROBERT. That's a really old card.
ABIGAIL. Yes, it is.
ROBERT. Let me see that. *(She hands it to him.)* That's from –
ABIGAIL. You gave it to me.
ROBERT. This's the first business card I had. I haven't seen that –
ABIGAIL. It's been a few years.
ROBERT. This is from when I first came to the city.
ABIGAIL. It's a cute card. I like the film strip logo.
ROBERT. Yeah. I did, too. They were very expensive.
ABIGAIL. But it only has this number.
ROBERT. Oh, right.

(Hands her a new card.)

ABIGAIL. *(She hands him another card.)* And here's mine.

(He's still holding the original card and they laugh at the tangle of hands and cards.)

ROBERT. Thanks.
ABIGAIL. *(Taking the old card from his hand.)* And this is mine.
ROBERT. *(Looking at her.)* Wow. Where did you get that?
ABIGAIL. You gave it to me.
ROBERT. I did?
ABIGAIL. On a bus.
ROBERT. A bus?
ABIGAIL. You don't remember?
ROBERT. Sorry, no.
ABIGAIL. That's okay.
ROBERT. Sorry.
ABIGAIL. No, *I'm* sorry.
ROBERT. Why?
ABIGAIL. You told me to call you for lunch. I never did.
ROBERT. I don't remember.
ABIGAIL. No reason you should.
ROBERT. But you do.
ABIGAIL. Well, I had the card. Otherwise I wouldn't –
ROBERT. Of course.
ABIGAIL. I don't think – anyway –
ROBERT. Of course not.
ABIGAIL. *(Embarrassed)* So, what about lunch? *(Pause)* I was supposed to call you for lunch. *(A beat.)* How about lunch at the Bear Cafe?
ROBERT. Well –
ABIGAIL. When I pick up the proofs.
ROBERT. Well, you don't have to –

ABIGAIL. I'd like to –

ROBERT. A bus? I met you on a bus?

ABIGAIL. Yes.

ROBERT. And gave you a card?

ABIGAIL. You started talking to me, we must have been sitting next to each other, you just started talking and gave me your card.

ROBERT. *(Pause)* So why didn't you ever call?

ABIGAIL. I think maybe I was dating someone, or something. I meant to call. I don't know. I meant to call a lot of times. I don't know. I don't know why I never did.

ROBERT. So why now?

ABIGAIL. Because I never did. And I wondered – well, I needed the pictures.

ROBERT. Right.

ABIGAIL. Procrastination.

ROBERT. What?

ABIGAIL. I put off calling.

ROBERT. *(Laughing)* For years?

ABIGAIL. I guess.

ROBERT. But you saved the card.

ABIGAIL. On my bulletin board. I put off that, too. Cleaning it. Just kept adding stuff.

ROBERT. Stuff.

ABIGAIL. Coupons, flyers, cartoons.

ROBERT. Business cards.

ABIGAIL. Just yours. I thought I'd run into you again.

ROBERT. On a bus.

ABIGAIL. I guess.

ROBERT. So.

ABIGAIL. So?

ROBERT. So, how've you been?

ABIGAIL. *(Laughing)* Fine, thanks, and you?

ROBERT. Great.

ABIGAIL. Good.

ROBERT. So.

ABIGAIL. Yeah.

ROBERT. Your work?

ABIGAIL. It's okay. You?

ROBERT. I've had a good business.

ABIGAIL. So I see.

ROBERT. Two kids.

ABIGAIL. You're kidding.

ROBERT. No.

ABIGAIL. *(Looking around.)* Where are they?

ROBERT. At the house.

ABIGAIL. And so you're –
ROBERT. Married. Right.
ABIGAIL. No ring.
ROBERT. *(Looking at his hands.)* I was printing before you came.
ABIGAIL. Printing?
ROBERT. Prints. You have to put your hands in –
ABIGAIL. Water.
ROBERT. Right. I made a closet and the bathroom into a darkroom. I mostly work in color, send stuff to the lab, but sometimes I do something on my own.
ABIGAIL. How long? How long have you –
ROBERT. Six years.
ABIGAIL. And it's good?
ROBERT. My life is very good. Yours?
ABIGAIL. Well, I'm still at the same place I was when I met you. Nothing's changed. Same apartment. Same scramble for jobs.
ROBERT. You seem good. Together.
ABIGAIL. I'm the same.
ROBERT. The magazine article?
ABIGAIL. Nothing important.
ROBERT. A trade magazine.
ABIGAIL. No, it's for my alumni magazine. They're doing an article.
ROBERT. That's good.
ABIGAIL. No, it's stupid. There's nothing to say. I'm the same.
ROBERT. That's okay.
ABIGAIL. No, I don't think so.
ROBERT. Why not?
ABIGAIL. Well, you, you're married. Kids.
ROBERT. Well, yes.
ABIGAIL. I didn't think –
ROBERT. What did you expect?
ABIGAIL. I don't know. Never mind.
ROBERT. No, what?
ABIGAIL. Never mind.
ROBERT. What did you expect?
ABIGAIL. It doesn't matter.
ROBERT. Yes, it does matter. You obviously expected something. You thought I'd be, what, available, when you finally, after ten years, want to have lunch?
ABIGAIL. That's not fair.
ROBERT. Yes, it is. Women complain that men never call, well?
ABIGAIL. You're lucky. To be married.
ROBERT. You have to take the opportunities when they're offered.
ABIGAIL. And I didn't.
ROBERT. Whatever.

ABIGAIL. I didn't expect anything. I'm just a blur. Not even.
ROBERT. What do you mean?
ABIGAIL. You're the camera. I crossed in front of your lens. But the film didn't see me.
ROBERT. No, the film sees. But it captures the bigger picture.
ABIGAIL. I really didn't expect anything.
ROBERT. That's not true.
ABIGAIL. I had just always wondered about you.
ROBERT. Well, my life turned out fine. And it probably wouldn't have been any different –
ABIGAIL. If what –
ROBERT. If you'd called. *(Pause)* We do what we're supposed to do. Get what we're supposed to get.
ABIGAIL. But opportunities.
ROBERT. You take the ones you're supposed to.
ABIGAIL. I don't know.
ROBERT. Maybe this is just a different opportunity. Maybe someone will see that picture in the magazine. Who knows what could happen. Wait. You've got something on ...

(Reaches to her cheek.)

ABIGAIL. What?
ROBERT. Wait, there, no, turn to the light.
ABIGAIL. What is it?
ROBERT. An eyelash?
ABIGAIL. Oh.
ROBERT. No, mascara, I think.
ABIGAIL. I'm not used to wearing this much make-up. Is it running?
ROBERT. No, it looks fine. Still looks fine.
ABIGAIL. Not that it matters.

(She gathers her bags.)

ROBERT. I think it always matters.
ABIGAIL. Thanks. Thanks for everything.

(She gets a scarf out of her bag.)

ROBERT. Call about the proofs.
ABIGAIL. *(Putting on the scarf.)* I will.
ROBERT. The scarf.
ABIGAIL. What?
ROBERT. You had a scarf.
ABIGAIL. Yes, in my bag.

ROBERT. On the bus. It was winter and you had a scarf. You had a big scarf. I complimented you on it.
ABIGAIL. Yes, you did.
ROBERT. It was a stupid thing to say, but I wanted to talk to you.
ABIGAIL. Yeah.
ROBERT. So we talked about the scarf.
ABIGAIL. I had forgotten –
ROBERT. That's how it started.
ABIGAIL. I remember.
ROBERT. I remember now. You didn't call, I didn't have your number, and I talked about the stupid scarf.
ABIGAIL. It was fine.
ROBERT. I remember now. I thought about you. I thought I'd run into you again.
ABIGAIL. And now we have.
ROBERT. You turned out okay.
ABIGAIL. Thanks. So did you.

(Pause)

ROBERT. Well, thanks for calling.

(They laugh.)

ABIGAIL. Thanks for the session.

(She is almost out the door.)

ROBERT. See you in ten years.
ABIGAIL. Right. I'm sorry I didn't call.
ROBERT. You should have. You should have called.

(Blackout. End of play.)

COSTUME PLOT

ABIGAIL: dress (or slacks with nice blouse), pumps or flats, sweater, jacket (in bag), clip-on earrings (in bag), scarf (in bag)

ROBERT: Khaki pants or jeans, t-shirt, demin or plaid flannel shirt, worn loose, sneakers or loafers

PROPERTY PLOT

stool

professional camera

tripod

small table or rolling cart

Polaroid film

loupe

a couple of chairs or a small sofa

professional Polaroid camera

light meter

35mm camera film

Polaroid pictures

professional photo lab envelope

other misc. camera equipment as set dressing

photographer's lights and umbrella (optional)

Robert's new business cards in a holder

photo lab business cards in a holder

bottles of mineral water

carry-on or large tote bag, containing jackets, earrings and scarf

purse containing compact, make-up, Abigail's business card and Robert's old card

FLOOR PLAN

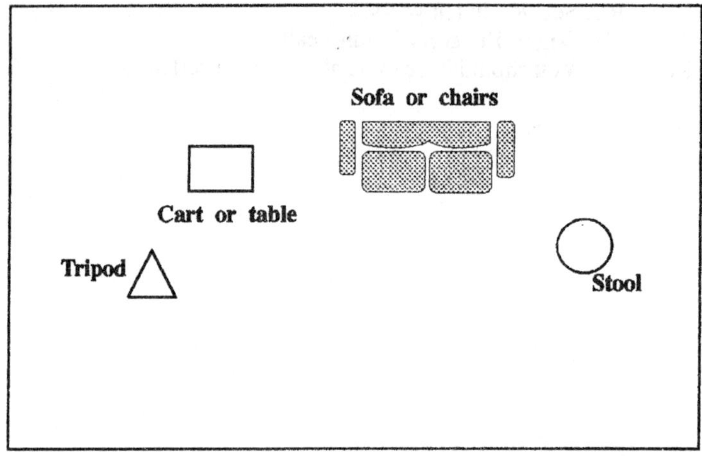

IT'S OKAY, HONEY

by

Bertha Brown

*Special thanks to Ron Hirt and Bill Swarts
for all their efforts with the short play festival
and for taking especially good care of me.*

Bertha

IT'S OKAY, HONEY

by
Bertha Brown

with

KELSEY . . . . Shelley Hunter

MOTHER . . . . Sue Glausen-Smith

Directed by Sharon Fallon

Produced by
Love Creek Productions, New York City

ABOUT THE AUTHOR

BERTHA BROWN is very happy to be a finalist in the Samuel French 23rd Off-Off Broadway Original Short Play Festival.

CHARACTERS

KELSEY: Age 17 or so
NANCY: Her mother, age 45 or so

SETTING

A contemporary suburban living room

KELSEY. *(On phone.)* Robert, it's not you. No, it isn't. It hasn't got anything to do with you. I like you. I want to be your friend. I'm just not interested in going on a date. I don't know about next month, but right now no, Robert. Listen to me very carefully. N.O. No. That's right. I'm turning you down. Goodbye.

NANCY. Honey, come over here and sit down.

KELSEY. Is something wrong?

NANCY. No, nothing's wrong, per se. I just thought we'd have a little chat.

KELSEY. Oh, brother.

NANCY. Now, what does that mean?

KELSEY. I remember some of our other chats.

NANCY. And?

KELSEY. Like when we had our drug chat.

NANCY. I thought that was very good.

KELSEY. Yes, but I ended up having to explain the difference between hash and crack to you.

NANCY. I'm glad you did that.

KELSEY. And that reefer, grass and marijuana were all the same thing.

NANCY. I know I should have been more prepared for our discussion on drugs, but my heart was in the right place, Kelsey. And you're not on drugs, are you?

KELSEY. No. No, I'm not.

NANCY. So, our little chat worked.

KELSEY. Whatever, Mother. But it's not just the drug chat. There was the sex chat.

NANCY. I know that embarrassed you, but you need to know these things, and you need to hear them from someone who cares about you.

KELSEY. It wasn't so much the talk, Mother. That was fine. I guess it's your obligation to do that. And I understand. But, well, it was the demonstration.

NANCY. Kelsey, I've read about these things, and that's what they do in the more progressive schools. And safe sex is important, and it's important that you know how to practice it.

KELSEY. Maybe. But for God's sake, Mother, where on earth did you ever find a cucumber that big? And that crooked?

NANCY. It was just meant to be a replica.

KELSEY. Well, I would hope not.

NANCY. You never know, Kelsey. Men come in all different shapes and sizes.

KELSEY. Well, all I know is you kept breaking the condom when you put it on the cucumber, and then you kept running into your bedroom and getting more and breaking them.

NANCY. I should have gone to the drug store and gotten the larger ones, but I didn't, and so I had to use your father's.

KELSEY. I'm sure Daddy would be proud you shared that with his daughter.

NANCY. At any rate, this isn't going to be that kind of talk.

KELSEY. Good. I think.

NANCY. I couldn't help overhearing you on the phone to Robert.

KELSEY. Yeah?

NANCY. And I couldn't help overhearing you turning him down for a date.

KELSEY. So?

NANCY. And during the past six months or so, I've heard you turn down date after date.

KELSEY. And your point is?

NANCY. Kelsey, I don't have a point.

KELSEY. But?

NANCY. Well, I just want you to know it's okay, honey.

KELSEY. I think I'm missing something.

NANCY. No, you're not missing anything. I mean it. It's okay, honey.

KELSEY. Well, good.

NANCY. It's going to take a bit of doing to bring your dad around, but don't worry. I can do it. And Kelsey, I want to be perfectly honest with you. I'm not going to tell you I'm not a little disappointed. I always wanted grandchildren when I got older. But it's okay, honey.

KELSEY. Mom. I have no idea what you're talking about.

NANCY. You always make me be the one to say it.

KELSEY. Say what?!?!

NANCY. Have it your way. You're just like your father. I'm saying that it's okay that you're a homosexual lesbian.

KELSEY. Whoa. Stop. Halt. Cease movement. Put on the brakes. Get out of the car.

NANCY. I knew this wasn't going to be easy.

KELSEY. Mother, listen to me. Listen to me very carefully. Are you listening?

NANCY. Yes dear.

KELSEY. I am not, I repeat, am not a lesbian.

NANCY. You don't need to be embarrassed, Kelsey. I read the newspapers and novels and, goodness, it's all over television these days, especially with that woman Ellen coming out of the closet. That's what it's called, right?

KELSEY. That's what it's called.

NANCY. In the past, it was something that people couldn't admit, Kelsey, but today, it's acceptable to be a homosexual lesbian.

KELSEY. Mother, that's lesbian. You don't say homosexual lesbian. You just need to say lesbian. It's redundant to say homosexual. That's a given. I don't think you could really be a homosexual lesbian. That'd be an oxymoron.

NANCY. Oh. Well, what if you were a lesbian but you were living with a man and having sex. What would you be?

KELSEY. Miserable, I guess. I don't know. But that's not what we're talking about. We're talking about me. And I am not a lesbian.

NANCY. But it's okay –

KELSEY. I know. I know. I understand that ... and I'm sure if I were a lesbian, Mother, I'd be happy that you feel that way. But I'm not. I don't have any lesbian tendencies that I'm aware of. I don't hate lesbians. It's fine if someone wants to be one. I'm just not someone who wants to be.

NANCY. Kelsey, sometimes it's not a matter of what you want. Sometimes that's just the way it is.

KELSEY. I know that. But it's not that way with me. I like males.

NANCY. If you like males, how come you don't go out with any?

KELSEY. Mother, a year ago you were concerned because I was going out all the time!

NANCY. But then you realized.

KELSEY. I realized that I was a promiscuous person and that I needed to get my life in control.

NANCY. But you were just trying to fit in.

KELSEY. I was doing a little more than trying to fit in, Mother. I was a very promiscuous person. You understand.

NANCY. You poor thing. You were just trying to make yourself be like the rest of your friends.

KELSEY. No, Mother! No, no, no. That's not it. Mother, I was what they called when you were growing up a "slut." Do you understand that? I was a slut. I was a slut, because I like men and I like sex. Do I need to be any clearer?!?

NANCY. You don't need to raise your voice, Kelsey.

KELSEY. Well, I don't know how else to make you understand.

NANCY. Let me ask you a question. Alright?

KELSEY. I guess.

NANCY. When you were experimenting with all these men, were you orgasming?

KELSEY. *(Embarrassed)* Mother!

NANCY. If you weren't, don't you see that you were just trying to be like everyone else, and your body was trying to tell you that you weren't?

KELSEY. Well, I did. I had orgasms. Not all the time. But most of the time.

NANCY. But not all the time.

KELSEY. No, not all the time. Do you have them all the time?

NANCY. That's different. I'm a married woman.

KELSEY. Mother, believe me, lesbianism is not my problem. Trust me.

NANCY. I just want you to be happy, honey. And I want you to know –

KELSEY. I know. I know. "It's okay."

NANCY. You know, honey, when I was a girl, a lot younger than you, I had this friend, Carol

KELSEY. Mr. Harding's wife?

NANCY. No. Carol doesn't live around here. She married and moved to Washington State. But as I was telling you. I had this friend, Carol. And when we were, oh, I don't know, 12, maybe 13, there was a time we spent experimenting.

KELSEY. Experimenting?

NANCY. With one another.

KELSEY. Mother, you don't have to tell me this.

NANCY. I'm not ashamed.

KELSEY. Well, good.

NANCY. We were experimenting with one another. Really little more than petting.

KELSEY. *(Under her breath.)* Oh, God.

NANCY. We'd fondle each other's breasts, and sometimes we'd lie together and move back and forth. You know what I mean.

KELSEY. I understand.

NANCY. We'd pretend that we were one of the other boys. We did that for quite awhile actually, one whole summer and into the fall. And then Carol got a crush on one of the boys in the class. I was really jealous at first. Felt like he was taking her away from me, then I got interested in someone and it all worked out in the end.

KELSEY. I'm glad it did, Mother.

NANCY. I just wanted to share that with you so you'd know that whatever you do, I'm here for you.

KELSEY. I know, Mother. And, Mother, I hope I don't have to call Robert back and make a date with him just so you'll believe me when I tell you I'm not gay.

NANCY. I believe you, honey. But if something should happen and you should decide –

KELSEY. Mother, it's not going to. I know I'm not a lesbian. I'm not so sure about you, but Mother. I just want you to know that I love you, and it's okay.

NANCY. *(Laughs)* Kelsey, you're just like your Dad. Got that mean sense of humor.

THE END

PROPERTY PLOT

Cordless Phone
Magazine
Coffee Cup

COSTUME PLOT

KELSEY:
Jeans, white t-shirt, flannel shirt, white sneakers.

NANCY:
Casual contemporary pantsuit.

FRANCIS BRICK
NEEDS NO INTRODUCTION

by

Jeff Hoffman

This play is for Harriet Hendlin,
with gratitude.

FRANCIS BRICK NEEDS NO INTRODUCTION was first produced as a staged reading at Abingdon Theatre Company on February 16, 1998. The cast, in order of appearance, was as follows:

BOBBY . . . . Allyn Burrows
JOE . . . . Moss Roberts
BRIAN . . . . Anthony Bertram
PETER . . . . Steve Deighan

The play was subsequently produced as part of the Samuel French Original Short Play festival. The director was Jackie Berger; the assistant director was Carol Johnson; Anthony Pappas was the stage manager. The cast, in order of appearance, was as follows:

BOBBY . . . . Anthony Sandkamp
JOE . . . . John Pszyk
BRIAN . . . . Anthony Bertram
PETER . . . . Steve Deighan

ABOUT THE AUTHOR

JEFF HOFFMAN was born in 1971 in Latrobe, PA. His poetry has appeared in journals throughout the country. In 1993, he won the Tom Williams Memorial Award in Poetry from the University of New Hampshire. His play, *Rubbernecking,* is a finalist for the 1998 Heideman Award from the Actors Theatre of Louisville. This is his first published play.

CHARACTERS

BOBBY BRICK: 29, the youngest brother. He has, of late, been on a bit of a Western music and clothes kick. He wears cowboy boots. He can usually get by with a joke and a wink. His brothers are a bit of a tougher crowd.

JOE BRICK: 30, a grad student in history now, but he previously worked on Wall Street. He left his fiancé, Gretchen, at the altar.

BRIAN BRICK: 38, a lawyer, genuinely likes the profession. He's a litigator and he's good at his job. No luck with relationships. A lot of luck with women.

PETER BRICK: 40, divorced, with a son, Jacob. His wife, Joan, has custody of Jacob.

The brothers' rivalries, as one might expect, are divided according to the gap in their ages. Bobby and Joe are very competetive as are Brian and Peter.

SETTING

    Place: The Brick family house. A big suburban house just barely outside a major city. The kitchen.

    Time: The present. During their father's wake.

(The Brick house is having a wake. In the kitchen, the four brothers are dressed in black. BOBBY isn't dressed as formally as his brothers. BOBBY wears cowboy boots.)
(PETER stands downstage left, apart from his brothers, looking into the crowd of people in the living room. BOBBY, JOE and BRIAN are sitting at the kitchen table, drinking. A bar with plenty of booze and a few crackers is upstage center, between PETER and his brothers.)
(As the lights rise, we hear a few bars of "Danny Boy" as the brothers hold in tableau for a few seconds. Gradually the music fades, and the brothers start to move.)

BOBBY. Pop drank.
JOE. Dad?
BOBBY. Dad. Yes. Dad drank.
JOE. Why'd you say Pop?
BOBBY. That's what I called him, *Joey*.
JOE. No you didn't, *Bobby*.
BOBBY. We all called him Pop.
BRIAN. Not me.
BOBBY. Bullshit.
JOE. Whata you from Texas ... from *Wy*oming?
BOBBY. Pop. I called him Pop.
JOE. Get the fuck outa here.
BOBBY. I think I know what I called my own father.
JOE. You didn't call him Pop.
BOBBY. I called him Pop!
BRIAN. Let's ask Peter.
BOBBY. Oh *fuck* this.
BRIAN. Peter, whatid Bobby call Dad?
BOBBY. Robert.
PETER. *(Distracted)* What?
BRIAN. Bobby here says he used to call Dad, Pop.
BOBBY. *Robert.*
PETER. He didn't drink.
BRIAN. What?
PETER. Didn't Robert say Pop drank?
BOBBY. Exactly. This is my freakin' point.
BRIAN. He's just quoting.
JOE. Who's quoting?
BRIAN. Peter is just quoting Bobby. "Pop drank." That's what Bobby
said. He doesn't mean we called him Pop or that he drank. Do you, Peter?

PETER. *(Distracted)* What?
JOE. Well, of course Dad drank, Brian. My point is –
BRIAN. Dad didn't drink.
JOE. Of course Dad drank.
BOBBY. Pop drank too.
BRIAN. Maybe he was drinking by the time he got to you two, but he wasn't drinking while Peter and I were there.
JOE. I find that hard to believe.
BOBBY. Pop was a boozer.
JOE. Hey Hank Williams, Jr., would you shut the fuck up?
BOBBY. I'm on your side here, Joey.
JOE. Joseph.
PETER. *(Looking into the other room.)* Mom's crying.
BRIAN. *(Joining PETER at the doorway.)* Who's she talking to?
PETER. I don't know him.

(BOBBY and JOE move over by PETER and look into the other room.)

BRIAN. Never saw him before. Nice suit.
JOE. That's Carl Adams. Her boss. An old man with a nice suit.
BOBBY. Slick. *(BRIAN, JOE and PETER look at BOBBY.)* What? That's what I call him. He's always wearing those Armani threads.
BRIAN. *(To BOBBY.)* Go sit down over there, cowboy.
BOBBY. What? Whatid I do?
BRIAN. Go sit down.

(BOBBY goes and sits down.)

PETER. So *that's* her boss.
JOE. Should we go out there?
BRIAN. He's hugging her.
PETER. She's crying. I never saw Mom cry before.
BRIAN. *(To PETER.)* She cried at your wedding.
JOE. We all cried at Peter's wedding. *(No response from PETER. He keeps looking at his mother.)* Sorry.
BRIAN. He's still hugging her.
PETER. But she *didn't* cry at my wedding. She likes Joan. She likes Joan more than she likes me.

(BOBBY goes to the bar.)

BOBBY. Drinks? Anyone need another beer?
JOE. Brewskis, you mean.

(BOBBY tosses JOE a bottle of beer.)

BOBBY. Bottle rockets, Joey. Bottle rocket, Brian?

BRIAN. Fire away, Robert.

BOBBY. *(As he tosses BRIAN a beer, referring to the "ROBERT".)* Thank you.

BRIAN. *(To PETER.)* Why didn't Joan come?

PETER. She couldn't get away.

JOE. From what?

PETER. From work.

JOE. What about Jacob? It's his grandfather.

PETER. I told her.

BRIAN. You asked her or you told her?

BOBBY. *(Sensing the tension.)* You want a beer, Peter?

PETER. No.

BRIAN. There's such a thing as taking a stand, Peter. Putting your foot down.

PETER. She raises my child, Brian. What do you want me to do?

(JOE joins PETER by the doorway again.)

JOE. *(Looking into the other room.)* Jesus, you're right. He got her a drink and now he's touching her elbow.

BOBBY. *(Coming over.)* Let me see this. ... That's an elbow. We definitely got elbow.

PETER. You can't blame her.

BRIAN. For what?

PETER. For the elbow.

JOE. What are you talking about?

PETER. Dad was no saint in the elbow department.

JOE. *What?*

PETER. Dad had an affair.

JOE. Get the fuck out of here. *Dad?*

BOBBY. I always wondered about that.

BRIAN. This is ridiculous. You're guessing, Peter.

PETER. I'm not guessing.

BRIAN. Whata you mean you're not guessing?

PETER. I mean I'm not guessing. He told me.

JOE. He *told* you?

PETER. He told me. Francis told me.

BRIAN. Francis?

PETER. Towards the end I called him Francis.

BRIAN. Let me get this straight you called our father *Francis* and he told you he had cheated on our mother.

BOBBY. I think that's what he's saying, Brian.

PETER. After Jacob was born, he told me he wanted to be ... friends. He told me to call him Francis.

BRIAN. Friends?

PETER. And after he found out about the cancer he started telling me things.

BRIAN. What things?

PETER. He told me he didn't ...

BRIAN. What?

PETER. He didn't really ...

BRIAN. What? *What?*

PETER. He didn't really like you very much.

BRIAN. I knew it. I knew it!

PETER. He loved you; he just didn't like you very much. What you did. Who you did it with.

BRIAN. He should talk!

PETER. It was one affair. It meant a lot to him, but it was one part of his life and then it was over.

BRIAN. I'm a lawyer. He was a lawyer. What the fuck more did he want?

PETER. He didn't like what he did. He hated his job. You reminded him of something he despised.

BRIAN. What did he want to do?

PETER. He wanted to be a fisherman.

BRIAN. Holy shit. Holy fuck.

(BRIAN sits down.)

JOE. *(Disbelief)* He cheated on Mom.

BOBBY. What did he say about me?

JOE. Bobby.

BOBBY. What? We find out he's had an affair; he doesn't like Brian. I wanna know what he said about me.

PETER. We didn't talk about you.

BOBBY. You didn't talk about me? Did you talk about Joey?

PETER. Yeah.

JOE. Whatid he say?

PETER. He said he respected you.

JOE. Well, there you go.

BOBBY. What for?

PETER. For not marrying Gretchen.

JOE. Thank you!

BOBBY. He gets respect for standing up Gretchen at the altar and I get nothing. How does that work?

JOE. Guess you just didn't make an impression.

PETER. Well, he said by the time Bobby came along he was all fathered out. He felt like he was phoning it in at that point.

(A quick salvage from BOBBY.)

BOBBY. So you did talk about me. That's all I wanted to know.

(BOBBY sits down beside BRIAN. JOE crosses to PETER.)

JOE. He never liked Gretchen, did he?
PETER. No, he liked Gretchen.
JOE. He just didn't think we belonged together ...
PETER. Yes ...
JOE. We were too different ...
PETER. Yes ...
JOE. I wanted to go to graduate school. She wanted me to stay on Wall Street.
PETER. He thought you were gay, Joe.
JOE. What?
PETER. He thought you were gay.
JOE. I HEARD YOU!
PETER. And I told him he was probably right.
JOE. You told him *what?*
PETER. You are gay, aren't you?

(Pause.)

JOE. Yes.

(JOE sits down beside BOBBY and BRIAN. There is a fairly long pause as the three younger brothers sip their drinks, and PETER continues to look at his mother. The pause should be long enough to make the audience aware of the solemn occasion behind all the sibling rivalry.)

PETER. Francis Brick was coughing his lungs away and he sat me down on the wicker chair on his porch – the porch he had let his youngest son repaint as a birthday present even though he didn't think it needed repainting and he hated yellow -- and he lit up a cigarette – because really, what did it matter anymore, even though his wife would have a fit if she saw and so he had to bribe the paperboy to deliver a pack rolled up in his morning paper, which he always got to first because he still got up an hour before his wife even though she still worked and he didn't anymore, which he was thankful for because he had hated his job for the last thirty years and if he had to guess he'd guess that that hate was what had given him cancer, not the cigarettes – because really didn't everything give you cancer, and if everything did then why not pick something important? Not cigarettes. Cigarettes weren't important. They were something to do when you weren't thinking about how you had managed to be perfectly miserable for eight hours a day for thirty years and sure it was because you loved your wife and you loved your kids but really what did it mean that love when you never told anyone who you really were and what you really thought. And sometimes on the holidays or at a wedding or a graduation you'd look around and see all your kids and their wives or girlfriends and your grandson and you'd sneak off in the corner where no one could see you but where you could see everyone and just for a moment you'd think you were a hero. You'd let yourself think that. Just real quick. Quietly. You'd sip a gin and tonic and just relax into it. And it would last until the drink was gone. And that was it. Back to work. You could never come to a conclusion. Because after all it wasn't a question of *was it worth it?* It wasn't a question at all. It was how you lived your life. What your life was like. A pattern. And wasn't that an achievement? Just the observation. Just that. Just knowing this was how you lived your life. This is what you did. No fooling around. No self-deception.

(PETER crosses to the bar and starts to fix himself a mixed drink.)

And then he'd get down to it.

Get a beer, he'd say. *I want to tell you something.*

And I would. I'd get a beer. And he'd say: Do you know your mother? You don't know your mother. Your mother is having an affair. Do I blame your mother? I don't blame your mother. Your mother is sixty-two years old and she is looking toward the future and when you are sixty-two you try to get yourself to look toward the future and you see how easy it is. And you should not blame your mother either because your father is a cheater and a liar and when he was diagnosed with cancer the second thing he did after he got seven other opinions is that he sat his wife down and told her the truth. Finally. And it seemed like a simple thing. Just to give an explanation. Just to say this is how I felt then and this is what I did. But now I feel this way and so this is what I do now. And it felt wonderful to tell her but of course it was impossible to explain. And you can understand this Peter, can't you, because you know about payback and you know about cheating. Because you had an affair and now you don't get to see your kid grow up. So I'm not going to explain anything to you, I'm just going to tell you what I did. What I thought.

I'd *appreciate* it, he said, if you'd stay and listen.

And I did. I stayed. And I came back and he talked some more and I drank some more beer.

(PETER crosses to the kitchen table and stands behind his brothers.)

So there you go. Francis Brick, our father, hated lawyers because he was a lawyer and it reminded him that he hadn't been brave enough to switch careers, and he respected Joe because he thought maybe he had told Gretchen the truth about himself and Bobby was a nice kid but he didn't know how to paint a goddamed porch. And Francis didn't have a drinking problem and we all called him different names.

(PETER finally sits down with his brothers at the table.)

And when he was done, he said: "See, isn't that great? Life doesn't usually get summed up so nice and clean for you, does it?"

I'll take that bottle rocket now, Bobby.

(BRIAN takes a beer from the bar and hands it to BOBBY. BOBBY passes it along to PETER. As PETER opens the beer and starts to drink, the brothers again freeze in tableau as the music swells and the lights fade.)

END OF PLAY

PROPERTY PLOT

Large kitchen table with six chairs, downstage right
    tablecloth
    empty beer bottles
    tray of crackers and cheese
Bar, upstage center
    various liquor bottles
    bottled beer
    whiskey tumblers
    shot glasses
    tray of crackers and cheese
Two chairs, downstage left

COSTUME PLOT

BOBBY: Dark-colored suit, western-style string tie, cowboy boots.

JOE: Dark-colored suit.

BRIAN: Dark-colored, expensive-looking suit, hair slicked back, Wall Street style.

PETER: Dark-colored suit.

FLOOR PLAN

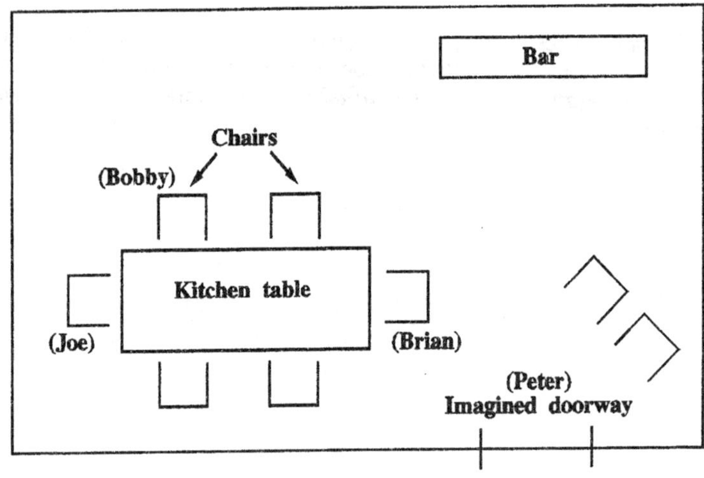

Off-Off-Broadway Festival Plays

**The best plays entered in the annual
Off-Off-Broadway Short Play Festival**

4TH SERIES

An Empty Space   Nothing Immediate   Open Admission

5TH SERIES

Batbrains   Me Too, Then!   "Hello, Ma!"

6TH SERIES

A Bench at the Edge   Seduction Duet

7TH SERIES

MD 20/20   Passing Fancy

8TH SERIES

Dreamboats   A Change from Routine   Auto-Erotic Misadventure

9TH SERIES

Now Departing   Something to Eat   The Enchanted Mesa
The Dicks   Piece for an Audition

10TH SERIES

Delta Triangle   Dispatches from Hell   Molly and James
Senior Prom   12:21 p.m.

11TH SERIES

Daddy's Home   Ghost Stories   Recensio   The Ties That Bind

12TH SERIES

The Brannock Device   The Prettiest Girl in Lafayette County
Slivovitz   Two and Twenty

13TH SERIES

Beached   A Grave Encounter   No Problem   Reservations for
Two   Strawberry Preserves   What's a Girl to Do

14TH SERIES

A Blind Date with Mary   Bums   Civilization and Its Malcontents   Do Over   Tradition 1A

15TH SERIES

The Adventures of Captain Neato-Man   A Chance Meeting Chateau Rene   Does This Woman Have a Name?   For Anne The Heartbreak Tour   The Pledge

16TH SERIES

As Angels Watch   Autumn Leaves   Goods   King of the Pekinese Yellowtail   Uranium   Way Deep   The Whole Truth The Winning Number

17TH SERIES

Correct   Address   Cowboys,   Indians   and   Waitresses Homebound   The Road to Nineveh   Your Life is a Feature Film

18TH SERIES

How Many to Tango?   Just Thinking   Last Exit Before Toll Pasquini the Magnificent   Peace in Our Time   The Power and the Glory   Something Rotten in Denmark   Visiting Oliver

19TH SERIES

Awkward Silence   Cherry Blend with Vanilla   Family Names Highwire   Nothing in Common   Pizza: A Love Story   The Spelling Bee

20TH SERIES

Pavane   The Art of Dating   Snow Stars   Life Comes to the Old Maid   The Appointment   A Winter Reunion

21ST SERIES

Whoppers   Dolorosa Sanchez   At Land's End   In with Alma With or Without You   Murmurs   Ballycastle

22ND SERIES

Brothers   This Is How It Is   Because I Wanted to Say Tremulous   The Last Dance   For Tiger Lilies Out of Season The Most Perfect Day

THE WAY TO MIAMI
by Donald Steele

HARRIET TUBMAN VISITS A THERAPIST
by Carolyn Gage

MERIDIAN, MISSISSIPPI REDUX
by Le Wilhelm

STUDIO PORTRAIT
by Arlene Hutton

IT'S OKAY, HONEY
by Bertha Brown

FRANCIS BRICK NEEDS NO INTRODUCTION
by Jeff Hoffman

SAMUEL FRENCH, INC.
45 West 25th Street, New York 10010-2751
7623 Sunset Blvd., Hollywood 90046-2795

IMPORTANT BILLING AND CREDIT REQUIREMENTS

All producers of THE WAY TO MIAMI, HARRIET TUBMAN VISITS A THERAPIST, MERIDIAN, MISSISSIPPI REDUX, STUDIO PORTRAIT, IT'S OKAY, HONEY and FRANCIS BRICK NEEDS NO INTRODUCTION *must* give credit to the Author(s) of the Play(s) in all programs distributed in connection with performances of the Play(s) and in all instances in which the title(s) of the Play(s) appears for purposes of advertising, publicizing or otherwise exploiting the Play(s) and/or a production. The name of the Author *must* also appear on a separate line, on which no other name appears, immediately following the title, and *must* appear in size of type not less than fifty percent the size of the title type.

OFF-OFF-BROADWAY FESTIVAL PLAYS
(Twenty-Third Series)

Selected by New York theatre critics, professionals, and the editorial staff of Samuel French, Inc. as the most important plays of the Twenty-Third Annual Off-Off-Broadway Original Short Play Festival, sponsored by Love Creek Productions.

TABLE OF CONTENTS